Down on the Farm

Down on the Farm

Childhood Memories of Farming in Canada

Jean Cochrane

FIFTH
HOUSE
PUBLISHERS

Front cover photograph, detail, Weaver children,
Lloydminster, SK, c. 1920. Courtesy McCord Museum,
Notman Archives, Montreal/8556

Back cover photograph, Children near Gleichen, AB,
c. 1900. Courtesy Glenbow Archives/NA-2157-1

Cover design by John Luckhurst/GDL

The publisher gratefully acknowledges
the support received from The Canada Council
and the Department of Canadian Heritage.

Printed in Canada by Kromar Printing Ltd.
96 97 98 99 00 / 5 4 3 2 1

CANADIAN CATALOGUING IN PUBLICATION DATA

Cochrane, Jean, 1932–

Down on the farm
ISBN 1-895618-80-0

1. Rural children - Canada - History. 2. Rural
children - Canada - History - Pictorial works.
3. Farm life - Canada - History. 4. Farm life -
Canada - History - Pictorial works. 5. Canada -
Rural conditions. 6. Canada - Rural conditions -
Pictorial works. I. Title.

S522.C3C63 1996   971'.009734083   C96-920075-7

FIFTH HOUSE LTD.
#9 – 6125 – 11th Street SE
Calgary AB Canada T2H 2L6

Contents

Introduction 1

The Family Farm 20

Women's Work 45

Illness and Injury 58

School 69

Community Life 101

Celebrations, Games,

    and Other Amusements 122

Hard Times

    and New Developments 143

End of an Era 156

References 169

Acknowledgements

I *WOULD LIKE TO THANK* those children of the farm who took time to tell the stories of their youth, and loaned me their pictures, both verbal and photographic. Their names are in the text. My thanks also go to: Anne Stewart of Calgary for introducing me to her farming family and friends, and for providing pictures; to Gwen Brathen Egan, Olive Murray Koyama, and Dorothy Mackenzie of Toronto for providing family photos and picture research; to Martha Moore, to Senior Link, Toronto, and to the Black Creek Pioneer Village, North York, for helping me to find people and pictures.

Thanks, of course, to the endlessly helpful archivists and curators in archives, museums, and libraries large and small, who provide access to the records of Canada's history. They included the Ontario Agricultural Museum and Archives, a resource that will soon no longer be publicly funded.

Introduction

C HILDREN OF THE FARM TRUDGE THROUGH THE history of this country, kicking up dust on the back roads, walking behind wagons to lighten the loads, squelching through fields to bring in the cows or plant potatoes, dawdling their way to school. They have been pioneers and contributors, junior partners in one of Canada's longest standing major industries, a vital part of a way of life that is virtually gone. The farm family was the primary agricultural production unit in Canada until the end of World War II brought in an era of rapid change that transformed the operation and economy of the business.

Farming was the way that thousands of families got their start in Canada, and from the beginning, all across the continent, children helped. They helped dig the hole in the ground for the first shack; they worked away from home to bring in a little needed cash, stock, or supplies; they stayed home from school to plant and harvest. Without their help it would have been harder to get a foothold in the wilderness, or to wrest a living from the self-sufficient family farm that nurtured Canadians for generations.

A family memoir describes how the Stockis began life in Canada: In 1907 the Stocki family, two adults and three children, made the long trip from Poland, and then the weary, lurching drive with a laden ox cart across the vast prairie countryside.

They were lucky. The eldest boy, at age fourteen, was already hired out to the priest in a village a few miles away. His father would drive into town every month to pick up his six-dollar wage.

They were doubly lucky. Twelve-year-old Joe was hired by a neighbour, a kindly, experienced settler from their home country.

If the boy would help him out with the stubborn oxen in his land clearing and stump pulling, he'd provide the family with grain, potatoes, and two young pigs. Besides, he'd see that the lad got some new, warmer clothing. He seemed to have outgrown and outworn everything he had brought along.

Alexander Stocki
Polish Pioneers of Good Faith and Bravery

The country itself grew up on the farm. In 1871, 80 percent of the population was rural—farmers and the people whose livelihood depended on them: millers, blacksmiths, village

Up through the 1930s, this is the way farms started in Canada, with a hole in the ground, and the labour of everyone in the family. ARCHIVES OF THE UNITED CHURCH OF CANADA, VICTORIA UNIVERSITY, TORONTO/93.049 P4272N

storekeepers, hired men—and agriculture accounted for 40 percent of Canada's gross domestic product. In the 1890s, with the railways in place, attracting farmers became a matter of national policy. They were needed to fill the country, its food baskets, and its rail cars, and the federal government's offer of virtually free land drew thousands of immigrants to western Canada, along with the restless and land hungry from other parts of the country. The wave of immigration lasted until the beginning of World War I, bringing about 2 ¼ million people into Canada and swelling the population to more than 7 million.

Not all of them, however, were rushing to plough the prairies. They were part of a population shift that foreshadowed what was to come. The inward wave of people overlapped a wave ebbing outward that took thousands of Canadians, notably from the Maritimes and rural Quebec, to cities in the United States. Many of them were leaving old farms that could not continue to support the whole family. And with southern Ontario and Quebec becoming increasingly urbanized and industrialized, and the new western towns thriving, Canada's own towns and cities attracted more than half the new immigrants, and were beginning to lure young people away from the farms.

The beckoning city and the dream of an easier life have always been blamed for the slow but steady decrease in rural population. It was a serious problem for the future of agriculture, and for individual farm families, who lost their best workers when the children left. The exodus became a plank in the political platforms of the farmers' parties that began to blossom in the teens and 1920s. Farm propagandists did everything they could to keep the young ones down on the farm. There were lessons in school and competitive

In a picture that was probably taken for the folks back home, this Ukrainian family poses proudly in their prosperous new home in Saskatchewan. ARCHIVES OF THE UNITED CHURCH OF CANADA, VICTORIA UNIVERSITY, TORONTO/92.195C

school fairs to teach farming techniques and to help lend the business an air of excitement. There were stories and poems and talks and sermons promoting the mythical image that still exists of the freedom, dignity, and virtue of life on the family farm.

In fact, the realities of that life helped make the bright lights look brighter. Even after the pioneer stage, they could include a twenty-four-hour work day, isolation and ignorance, primitive living conditions, and unceasing, exhausting demands on time and strength. Until the use of machinery and electricity became widespread, even on well-established farms, life was both labour intensive and cash short. Children started work young—from the time they could collect eggs or carry kindling—and kept at it until they left, virtually indentured to their parents until they were adults. And the end of childhood came early, as they took on heavier responsibilities: "We just learned how to do the things. When you'd get to be fourteen years old, you'd be grown up."

"As the younger boys became strong enough to carry a stick of wood, they joined the elder . . . It established early in life a principle of independence that what they receive is the reward of industry." (LtCol. Wm. T. Baird, 1890, *Seventy Years of New Brunswick Life*)

On the other hand, a farm is not only a place to work, it is home, with all the ties and emotions that conjures. Farm children grew up loved and loving, proud that they could

There were still corduroy roads near Clear Prairie, British Columbia, in about 1930. This mailman is giving a lift to someone from the Sunday School Caravan Mission, and to the man beside him, who had sixty miles to travel to get home from the hospital. ANGLICAN CHURCH OF CANADA GENERAL SYNOD ARCHIVES/P8005-25

builder—a duty owed to parents and a sure way to keep the young out of trouble. Grim little axioms about hunger being the best sauce, and a general gloomy conviction in some circles that children were born with a burden of original sin, and it was up to them to work it off, justified putting children to work in all sorts of capacities. If parents needed further encouragement, an 1882 royal commission report on factory conditions included the comment that children were better off working than running the streets.

The type of work depended on who the children were. Only the children of the wealthy would not have chores to help, pleased to feel that they were useful. And not all of them found the work onerous. Many of them enjoyed the animals, enjoyed watching things grow. Many grew up to be farmers themselves, who had learned their trade from proud parents. Besides, they were not the only children who worked. Though the need for child labour lingered longer on the farm than it did in other settings, children worked as a matter of course in nineteenth and early twentieth century Canada. When so much was done by hand, there was plenty for them to do, and work was considered a moral muscle

A soldier home from World War I probably let the young fry get on with the job of stacking all this firewood properly. MARY BURTON, VELLORE, ONTARIO

do, and even they were sometimes pressed into service as a matter of principle. For the comfortably well off in towns and cities, work was a training exercise and familial duty. It might mean sifting ashes, helping to care for animals, or running errands. Further down the social and economic scale was the hidden workforce of children who were, like farm children, unpaid contributors to a family business. Children of store owners worked behind the counter, stocked shelves, swept out. If Mother ran a boarding-house or did piece-work at home, children helped. Children brought in cash by selling newspapers; they were delivery boys and part-time domestics. The poorest shined shoes, sold boot laces and fruit on the streets, scavenged for scrap to sell and for necessities such as coal or wood to take home.

The royal commission found 2,261 children under fourteen working in factories and mines from Ontario to Prince Edward Island, and one of its recommendations was that their work week be reduced to sixty hours. There was a spattering of this kind of regulation in the 1880s and 1890s, largely unenforced, and easily circumvented. No similar regulations were applied to farm or family labour.

As late as 1911 the census showed more than twenty-five thousand children between the ages of ten and fourteen gainfully employed. About half the girls were working as domestics. There were children apprenticed to learn trades, and working in Canada's retail businesses, factories, and mines. Though the scale was never as large as in older

Horses were hard-working friends on farms. Children learned to ride and drive them early, and to make sure they were groomed and well fed. MULTICULTURAL HERITAGE CENTRE, STONY PLAIN, ALBERTA

industrialized countries, it was an appalling life for any child.

Fortunately for these children, however, the late nineteenth/early twentieth century was an era of social reform. The so-called "child savers" were putting in place the foundations of social services and legislation that would benefit children. They worked through churches and voluntary groups that would evolve into children's aid societies and government social service agencies. And major women's organizations such as the Women's Institutes and the Na-

tional Council of Women were beginning their work, which would include the welfare of children. But the focus of the early reformers was urban, and concentrated on industrial and commercial workplaces, on homeless street urchins and visible, obvious abuses.

In the countryside, unnoticed by reformers or census takers, there were more children working than those born to the farm. There was an informal exchange of children, loaned or hired out as part of a floating labour pool, that satisfied a number of needs. If a family had too many mouths to feed, it would send a child to help out at a neighbour's or a relative's farm in return for bed, board, and perhaps some payment in kind. Or a child might be sent away from home for the sake of opportunity, in hopes of trading labour for schooling, training, or experience of a wider world, away from the isolation of a homestead. Women took in girls from poorer families, often immigrants, to help in the house. In return, the girls learned domestic skills and Canadian ways and languages, all designed to make them more marketable as wives or workers.

Gavin Green, loaned out to a farmer to ease the load on the family income, was made to feel the social stigma of being a hired boy, though he clearly didn't suffer much otherwise:

I had lots of chores to do, as the boss and his hired man teamed wood to Goderich every day. I was well fed, but lonesome. The daughter would not play with her father's chore boy, so I had to play by myself when I got my work done.

I was at this place about six weeks when I got fired. One morning when I came up for breakfast, the mistress said to me, "Take that grease and grease Amelia's shoes." I said, "I will not." "Well, then get your breakfast and go home." The word home sounded good to me.

At a second posting he had to share a bed with a bearded, hairy, hired man, and work hard at looking after the cattle, but he got his reward.

When the haying had to be done, mother brought the infants along to keep an eye on them while she worked.

Mr. John Quaid came down to our home at Morrish's Mill leading a two-year-old steer as a present to me for staying on the job, pulling the straw out of the stack to feed the cattle, and doing what Mrs. Quaid told me to do and being a good boy and not saying bad swear words to the cattle or driving them to water with a pitchfork. I felt as big and important as Big Bill McLean, the cattle buyer of Goderich. I was some drover.

The Old Log School and Huron Old Boys in Pioneer Days

Mabel and Clarence Reid on their way to feed the pigs in the Cremona area of Alberta, 1915. GLENBOW ARCHIVES/NA-1930-2

from Canada's own pool of orphaned and neglected children. An advertisement in the June 15, 1897, issue of *The Farmer's Advocate* offered the services of English "home" boys from the best known of the placement agencies.

The Managers of Dr. Barnardo's Homes will be glad to receive applications from farmers or others for the boys whom it is proposed to send out from England in several parties during the coming season. All the young immigrants will have passed through a period of training in the English Homes, and will be carefully selected with a view to their moral and physical suitability for Canadian life. Full particulars as to the terms and conditions upon which the boys may be placed may be obtained on application to Mr. Alfred B. Owen, Agent, Dr. Barnardo's Homes, 214 Farley Ave., Toronto.

There were other children who could not go home if they were unhappy. They were the children imported wholesale from England's backstreets and orphanages, and others

If not roaming the streets, Canada's homeless and deserted children competed for cold berths as domestics and unskilled labour. The rationale was that they were learning something that would guarantee them a way to make a living.

The children were not all cruelly treated, but there was little of Anne of Green Gables about it, either. Pulled from their roots and sent, where chance would take them, to work alone among strangers, they would suffer from loneliness and lack of affection, from being different, and from knowing that no one really cared about them beyond what work they could do. There was a sharp dividing line in attitude towards these young waifs and children who had known families and backgrounds. They were strangers of unknown heritage, alone and unprotected, cheap labour.

The agencies imported about eighty thousand children from the 1860s to the late 1920s, and lingered, under increasingly widespread social disapproval, until the 1940s. Supervision was difficult and unsatisfactory, and though some of the children were adequately or even kindly cared for, others suffered terrible abuses—overworked, underfed and poorly clothed, and socially shunned. Two English boys in Ontario killed themselves in 1924. Only one of the farmers involved was charged. Incredibly, a study conducted at the time by the Social Service Council of Canada on Canada's child immigrants said, "It may be argued that it is not the nature of a normal child of British stock to take his own life, even under the strain of severest cruelty . . . Either of them could have run away, as others in similar straits have done."

Farmers were prime clients for both the agencies and the orphanages, and one of the justifications for this bustling trade in children was the claim that they would benefit from

In 1904, four generations of William Castator's family posed in front of their log house in Vaughan, Ontario. Log houses might be added onto for years before they were replaced by something better. CITY OF VAUGHAN ARCHIVES/M993.20 VOL. 1

the special virtues of farm life. J.J. Kelso, a leading Canadian child saver, wrote in 1910:

Many of our brightest and cleverest public men were born on the farm and spent their early days in the country. This is one reason why we desire to get our

A tough decision for judges at the school fair in Vellore, Ontario, in 1930. CITY OF VAUGHAN ARCHIVES/MG1 VOL. 1

homeless boys and girls away from the crowded city institutions to the free and healthy life of the farm. The children in the country enter into all the social activities of the home and are happy in the feeling of companionship and equality. Their help is prized, and, learning to work, they grow strong and self-reliant, able in later life to take their share valiantly in the world's great workshop. If our friends in the country will help the children while they are young, they will in turn lend their aid when older. Remember, however, always to treat them justly, for a child's sense of justice is keen and unerring.
– from *Children, Their Care, Training and Happiness as Future Citizens*

Before the establishment of effective adoption laws, there were also extra children on farms as a result of simple acts of kindness, when farm families informally, almost casually, adopted children who had problems at home, or whose parents had died. But even then it was assumed that the children would be trained for something: "In the 1930s we took in a cousin for a few years when her parents died, and Mom found a place for her where she could work and go to school when she was about fifteen."

These temporary additions often became accepted as members of the family: "Mother and Dad looked after a boy

John Ware's young family pioneered in Alberta at the turn of the last century. NATIONAL ARCHIVES OF CANADA/C37966

This Bukovinian mother and daughter, living near Vegreville, Alberta, were photographed in their national dress for an article in the January 1911 *Canadian Pictorial* magazine. Bukovina is in Ukraine.

who belonged to a friend of theirs who had remarried. There were too many kids, and they didn't have a farm. The father asked if he could come and stay on the farm, and he did, and helped Dad one spring. Then he went away and came back. He was just as much a brother as my brothers."

The work done by hired children was not always any harder than that expected of the family's own. Necessity made its demands, and farm children accepted responsibility as a fact of life. Forgetting meant animals that hadn't been fed or watered on time, vegetables that hadn't been hoed, or no firewood or water in the house at dinner-time. Consequences could be swift and painful. Generally the children accepted the responsibilities and the chores patiently enough; everyone they knew was in the same boat. It was a way of life.

We all had our own chores. As far back as I can remember, it was my job to keep the woodbox full for Mom. One time I kept putting it off and didn't do it. The next day Dad made me get in fifteen loads of wood. When my brother did the same thing, Dad went upstairs at night and woke him up and made him fill the box. You've got to learn to be responsible. (Margaret Dixon, Parkman, Saskatchewan)

The amount of work might seem daunting to a contemporary child: "We had chores to do, and we were responsible for them. When I got home from school I was to get the cows

Following in his father's footsteps wasn't really child's play, but this boy's help was needed. One person and one horse could plough about an acre in a day with a hand plough. ARCHIVES OF THE UNITED CHURCH OF CANADA, VICTORIA UNIVERSITY, TORONTO

Some loved the life: "I got a kick out of the whole works. There were some jobs you didn't like—I didn't like cows. But the horses were a kind of hobby."

Others hated it: "The cows were a mile in that direction, and the mail a mile in the other, and I had to get them both. We worked all day long. I was tired when I was a kid; I never felt like a young person. I've always been old and tired, ever since I was eight years old, I think." (Frances Davey, Cobourg, Ontario)

in, feed the pigs, milk the cows, and separate the milk."

Occasionally a neighbour would hire a child for the day. The prospect of earning money was always attractive.

When our neighbour was expecting company, she would send over for one of the girls, and you'd work all day, cleaning brass and the like, and if you got twenty-five cents, that was big. (Esther McDonell, Enfield County, Nova Scotia)

But despite all this, the fact is that all of the children did not work all of the time. Those who did, tended to be crisp about those who didn't: "Made you mad sometimes. My cousin next door didn't have anything to do, and that used to gall me." (Arnold Bent, Belleisle, Nova Scotia)

My older sister and I did a lot of work on the farm. My second oldest sister, Mother said she wasn't well. There wasn't anything the matter with her that I could see. She weighed more than any of us. (Cecilia Murphy, Read, Ontario)

My brother Alec never did a damned thing. Brushed his own teeth, I guess. (Anna Murray, Earltown, Nova Scotia)

"I had very kind parents, and a brother who was eight years older. I liked walking in the rain, and going to get the cattle. We were five miles from Rimbey, Alberta, and I liked going to town on a Saturday night. I didn't know I was lonely. We didn't know anything else." (Maxine Keith, Rimbey, Alberta)

Some took time to smell the flowers:

June, and the prairie covered with flowers, grass a foot long, sleek well-fed cattle everywhere. I rode up to the nine mile butte at the head of the lake one evening to get tiger lilies. It was beautiful, the plains stretching away to the Eastward, the belly buttes tall and sort of purple to the Southward, and behind me the Porcupine Hills and the sun going down. (Nina Grier, Macleod, Alberta)

Some, as a mischievous paragraph in the July 13, 1887 *Christian Guardian* suggests, just plain goofed off:

There are so many bright spots in the life of a farm boy that I sometimes think I should like to live the life over again. I should almost be willing to be a girl if it were not for the chores. There is a great comfort to a boy in the

For generations, farm children stayed home from school in the fall to help harvest, although, in 1898, there may not yet have been a school in the neighbourhood for these boys. ARCHIVES OF THE UNITED CHURCH OF CANADA, VICTORIA UNIVERSITY, TORONTO

amount of work he can get rid of doing. It is sometimes astonishing how slow he can go on an errand. Perhaps he couldn't explain himself why, when he is sent to a neighbour's after yeast, he stops to stone the frogs. He is not exactly cruel, but he wants to see if he can hit 'em. It is a curious fact about boys that two will be a great deal slower in doing anything than one.

The beginning of the end of this way of life came not only from the competition of towns and industries, but from changes on the farm itself. They were signalled in the 1870s, when the first mammoth threshing-machine lumbered through a farm gate, and more clearly a few decades later, when the first tin Lizzie rattled into a mud-hole. A crop it formerly took weeks to harvest could be brought in more efficiently in days. A village an hour away by horse was five minutes away by car, and the city not much farther.

People worried for years about the drift of young people away from the farms, though it

By horse and buggy it could take a long time to drive to the nearest village, and children didn't get there very often. MCCORD MUSEUM, NOTMAN ARCHIVES, MONTREAL/3596

was natural enough. Even before they were mechanized, farms could only support so many people, and as the country grew, more options became available. But publications such as *The Farmer's Advocate* scolded their readers, urging them to make farm life more comfortable and interesting for their children. An 1893 editorial, pleading the case for education to improve the farm and keep young people interested, offered the following advice:

Our young people will learn that there is something more than plod in farm life; that there is a wide field for

Farm children learned to make their own amusements, like these two in Gladys Ridge, Alberta, in the late 1920s. ANNE STEWART, ALBERTA

the exercise of their intellectual being, and that the farmer's or the farmer's wife's life can be as respectable as that of any other man or woman who breathes the air of heaven. Some of the future results will be: Fewer of our boys leaving the farm; fewer of our girls preferring the stylish dude to the substantial, noble-minded agriculturalist; agriculture placed where it ought to be, as the most independent and honorable calling open to men and women, which God speed the day.

–from "Why the Boys Leave the Farm," June 1, 1893

Stylish dudes had nothing to do with it in most cases:

I left home when I was about twenty. I couldn't stand the farm. I didn't like it; it was too hard work. After Mother died, my sister and father ran the farm, and she said, "You're not going to get paid for anything you do. If you need a pair of shoes, you'll have to buy them yourself." I don't know where she thought I'd get the money. I went to Toronto. I told them I was going to Belleville.

The Farmer's Advocate waged a relentless campaign to encourage youngsters to stay on the farm. In 1919, nearly thirty years after "Why the Boys Leave the Farm," the paper was still at it, this time admonishing "Mr. Rural" for his lack of foresight.

To use his father's words, he has got to be "pretty handy around the place." Being a willing, besides handy worker, his father sees to it that there are few idle moments, until some day the boy awakens to the fact that he's being robbed of time to play; this play time is supposed to be when his work is done, but so very often the end of his day's work is perilously near bed time . . . He rebels. One thing leads to another, and sooner or later you'll see him "hiking" for where the smoke hangs low in the sky. Will he come back? Generally speaking, no.

Handling horses and the heavy farm sled was just part of the day's chores for farm children. MULTICULTU-RAL HERITAGE CENTRE, STONY PLAIN, ALBERTA

ingly pipe to his financial hearing, "Where's Bill? Where's Lillie?—Gone?"
–from "Why Mr. Rural Loses His Children,"
April 10, 1919

While farmers fought the social changes that challenged their traditions and their collective influence on society, at the same time they were welcoming the new equipment, the telephones and radios, and the improved roads, which significantly raised their living standards. They began to buy clothes, and even food, in town or from the catalogue, instead of making it all at home. That altered the economics of the family. The upkeep of children began to cost money.

The Depression of the 1930s and the shortages of World War II slowed the process, but inexorably, a different world took shape. The 1941 census showed there were still 3 million of Canada's approximately 11.5 million people living on farms, about 80 percent of which were family owned. But the real transformation was just around the corner. By 1945, few farms and farmers were completely isolated. The children

The leaven of change, however, works but slowly in Mr. Rural's mind, and doubtless the seasons will pass, many of them, before he actually realizes that his young people need a little more time for recreation than he is allowing them; need the better schools which, with his eye on taxes, he doesn't attempt to secure for them, need some place where, in comfort, they could read or play, or argue to their heart's content. [Until he does] so long shall the robin each spring-time plaintively and question-

went into town every day for school. Farms got bigger, more expensive, more productive; there was more machinery indoors and out. In 1900, one farm worker supplied five people. By 1941, it was ten, and by 1962, the number had risen to thirty-one. The era of the nearly self-sufficient family farm passed, and there was no longer as much for young hands to do.

Attitudes to children and childhood had also changed by this time. Children were expected to stay in school longer and start work later. The farm child who once left school at the end of grade seven or eight, now needed an education to manage the chemistry, the husbandry, the equipment, the marketing and finances of a farming business. But it took some time to happen. From a child's eye view, the basics of life on a family farm remained much the same from the 1880s until the 1940s.

To get a feel for it, you need to slow to the pace of a walking horse, dim the lights in the house and barn to flickering lanterns, roll back the pavement, and distance the larger world, back to when a farmer had to go to town for the mail and the news.

Agriculture was one of Canada's major industries when it was prominently featured in this archway put up in Dundas, Ontario, for a visit by Prime Minister Sir John A. Macdonald. ARCHIVES OF ONTARIO/2457 S6 936

"News travelled slowly," said Cecilia Murphy, who was born in eastern Ontario in 1903. "If you had to give a message, you'd have to take the horse and buggy. When World War I broke out, Dad heard about it because he was in town, and that's how we found out." When it ended on November 11, 1918, an age-old style of signalling sent the word to six-year-old Morris Silbert, living on a farm near Hamilton.

We were home from school that day, helping to pick potatoes, and we could hear the factory whistle in the city which was twelve miles away, and somebody rang the school bell for a solid hour, and that really left an impression that the war was over.

That kind of isolation didn't end until the 1920s and 1930s, when telephones and radios broke the silence. It was a life that extended a few miles in each direction, lived largely among a few neighbours, brightened by visiting, by church, school, and the occasional excitement of fairs or school concerts. It was a life that helped to shape Canada. As this century turns, only about 4 percent of Canadians are farmers, and they operate in a different world.

The pig looks a bit surprised, as Alberta farm child and photographer exercise a sense of humour. ANNE STEWART, ALBERTA

The Family Farm

MORNING CAME EARLY FOR FARM CHILDREN, SIG-nalled by the clatter of the kitchen stove as Mother or Dad started the fire. "I got up about 5:00 in the summertime. We had to have chores and breakfast done and be in the field by 7:00." (Clarence Read, Carvil, Ontario) They got to sleep a little later in the fall and winter: "You'd get out there at 8:00 in the morning on a November morning and maybe have ten acres to do, furrows about eight inches wide. You could do two acres in a day. It was a lonely feeling." (Gordon Bennett, Carlisle, Ontario)

In the winter, the fire made the kitchen the only place in the house that would ever get really warm, and even that took a while, so they'd snug back down for a few minutes in a nest of straw and siblings. "We had lots of heavy bed clothes, but you could see frost on the nails in the winter, and there'd be hoarfrost on the blankets and your eyelashes." (Nazla Dane, Indian Head, Saskatchewan)

"We slept three in a bed, and the one in the middle was sometimes the only warm one. You'd be afraid to sleep alone because you never slept in a room by yourself. I didn't know anybody that had just one child." (Esther McDonell, Enfield County, Nova Scotia)

Even at dawn, there were children ready to welcome the day. "It was quiet in the morning, if you weren't in the barn. We had the Gaspé mountains, the most beautiful scenery you could ever want. I can remember waking up at 5:00 in the summer and watching the sun come up and seeing my Dad already out on the water, fishing." (Florence Thompson, Black Point, New Brunswick)

> "We had cotton ticks, and every time they threshed, we'd fill them up, and you'd make a little dent in that straw mattress and crawl in. By the time you'd get fresh straw, it would be all crumbled down and dusty. We didn't know what comfort was in those days." (Grace Arthur, Alnwick Township, Ontario)

The daily life of a family farm had some constants, whether it was a Nova Scotia apple farm, an Ontario dairy farm, or a Prairie homestead. The average size ranged from three hundred acres down to fifty. The smaller farms were common in the Maritimes and eastern Quebec, where many farmers doubled as fishermen.

Once out of the straw tick, a quick splash of face and hands in cold water, a trip to the outhouse, maybe emptying your chamber-pot, and it was chore time. Where basic outdoor chores were concerned, there wasn't much division

Cleaning out the barn was a low-skill job that the very young could help with. Toodie and John Bolton pose here with their pitchforks on the family farm in Alberta. ANNE STEWART, ALBERTA

around to feed them. You had to see that they had water out in the yard and clean out the hen-house. You'd take a fork and clean out the manure, take and put it out in the yard, then go and get fresh straw and put it in the nests and on the floor. In the wintertime we would throw the feed in the straw and they'd have to scratch for it for exercise. (Frances Davey, Cobourg, Ontario)

I remember having to crawl way back under the barn to find eggs because that's where the blamed hens would go, and that would make me so disgusted. (Grace Arthur, Alnwick Township, Ontario)

My cousins and I laugh over our favourite memory. Our grandmother would say, "How would you like to fill the woodbox? How would you like to gather the eggs?" I've never really liked chickens; I hated going into the barnyard with all those chickens pooping everywhere. I'd rather fill the woodbox. (Margaret Crawford, Erieau, Ontario)

between boys and girls; anyone could do them. Age and size and strength made the differences.

The youngest might stay indoors to help get breakfast or load up the kindling box, while the middle ones slopped the pigs and looked after the hens. Children didn't like chickens much; they were too much trouble.

You'd go open the barn and get the grain and spread it

One farm girl complained that she didn't like feeding birds because they were so greedy and had mean little eyes. The Nick Hucal family is assembled here on their farm southeast of Fisher Branch, Manitoba, in 1928. PROVINCIAL ARCHIVES OF MANITOBA, ANDREW MALOHE COLLECTION 10/N5486

after both. "You'd learn to milk very early, because we always had twenty or so cows. It took about fifteen minutes a cow, depending on how fast you could strip them. We had one that was a kicky cow. Sometimes she'd knock you right off the stool. I did break my toe once because they were fighting, and I kicked one." (Cecilia Murphy, Read, Ontario)

In the winter there was water to be carried in for them, and feed to be forked down from above. The rest of the year the cows were let out to loaf around in the pasture for the day, but they left lots of work behind them, so to speak. The barn had to be shovelled out morning and night, and the manure added to the pile, where eventually it could be shovelled again, to be spread on the garden or a field. Then the cattle had to be bedded up with fresh, clean straw, and the milk had to be processed through the separator.

Eventually, you got even with the chickens. "In November and December and January they didn't lay many eggs, but that was when they tasted best." (Frances Davey, Cobourg, Ontario)

When you were a little older, your day started in the dark, high-smelling barn, feeding the horses, ideally, an hour before they started work, milking the cows, and cleaning up

In 1912, E.A. Wharton Gill wrote a first-person, fictional account of the life of a Manitoba Chore Boy, published by the Religious Tract Society in London. The boy's unrelentingly cheerful attitude was meant to encourage real young people to follow in his footsteps. At seventeen, he would have been an old chore boy, working beside the young son and daughter of his employer, but the descriptions of how he learned are real enough.

Even nondairy farms kept a few cows. It took about fifteen minutes to milk a cow, even when she was co-operative. ESTATE OF A.S. MURRAY, P.E.I.

Little Ben and I go out first to the stables and feed the cows and clear out the cows' stalls while Mr. Gregory attends to the horses. Mrs. Gregory and Little Ben milk the cows between them. As soon as I can milk properly, Little Ben and I are to do all the milking. At present I am learning to milk on what they call a "stripper," that is a cow which only gives a little milk, and which they will stop milking altogether soon. I am managing pretty well now, but for the first few times, I got very tired of the performance, and so did Old Molly, the cow.

Then the milk was processed: "All the new milk is put through a thing called a 'separator.' It is worked with a big wheel and a handle, and I turn the handle while Mrs. Gregory attends to the milk and the cream. It takes about half an hour, but it is hard work while it lasts." The separator had to be taken apart and washed, night and morning, seven days a week. "I hated drying the separator," said Maxine Keith of Rimbey, Alberta, remembering the thirties. "My mother made me wash every disc separately, twenty-six or twenty-seven of them. A lot of people would just kind of swish them around."

Finally, with the barnyard temporarily tidy and quiet, it was time for breakfast and the trek to school if you weren't working at home. But it all began again, with variations, in the afternoon. "When you came home from school, there were lots more chores to do. You didn't get too much time for sleigh riding." (Clarence Read, Carvil, Ontario)

"We came home from school and filled the woodbox. The well was up the hill, and if our wooden pipe wasn't working, we'd have to go up the hill and get a pail, or go to the neighbours. Growing up on a farm you have so much to do you don't have time to run around and get into mischief. We liked to work. We had to work. If we complained, it didn't do much good." (Grace Arthur, Alnwick Township, Ontario)

The farm was as close to self-sufficient as could be. Dad worked in the fields and barns, Mother cooked and preserved, kept the kitchen garden, and made most of the clothes and bedding. Whatever the main crop, the farm would have a few cows, a pig or two, some chickens, and several horses. It would probably grow enough feed for the animals. "Father's maxim was feed what you grow, and grow what you feed."

Cash, which was scarce, would come from crops, from father's winter work off the farm, mother's eggs and butter, and whatever a child could raise, perhaps by hiring out, caretaking at school, or selling subscriptions to neighbours. The money was used for operating necessities and for supplies you couldn't grow, such as kerosene or sugar.

Hired men were expensive for small farmers and were often transients, taken on when there was heavy work that called for adult strength. In good times they were scarce because there were other jobs available. But even on farms where there were long-term hired men, there were chores that belonged just to the children—chopping kindling, weed-ing, picking stones, feeding those chickens—with the sun, the wind, and the weather shaping the work that changed to meet each season.

There was water to carry in, and wood to chop and carry. Said George Walker, in British Columbia, "The first thing my father ever gave me, when I was seven, was a hatchet. There were ten kids and I was the oldest. Chop wood, chop wood,

When the girls got through helping to harvest the fruit, they worked with their mother to turn it into pies, jam, and preserves for the winter.
PUBLIC ARCHIVES OF PRINCE EDWARD ISLAND, MILLIE GAMBLE COLLECTION/2667/134

Jack Barkley, four, in Alberta's Twining district about 1912. Farm children are never too young to feed the hens. GLENBOW ARCHIVES/NA-2299-10

all the bloody time. My mother was always after me to have enough kindling to start the fire in the morning."

There were gardens to tend, a major source of food both winter and summer. In the spring, under Mother's eye, the children helped to plant them. In the summer they kept them hoed and weeded, and in the fall helped to dig them up for storage and preservation. "We had about five big gardens. Mostly we dug the ground up by hand with a spade. We put rows in for vegetables and potatoes, turnips, carrots, peas and beans, cucumbers, corn. We had a big patch of strawberries; we'd have a dishpan full every other day." (Ben Goodwin, Cape Sable, Nova Scotia)

In some gardens, the stones seemed to grow even faster than the weeds: "I had to get every damn stone out of the garden," said George Walker. "You'd take a bucket and pile them up. Eventually there was a pile of stones there fifteen by ten feet and four or five feet high, and every one of those stones I put there." Cecilia Murphy said they used them for fences in eastern Ontario: "Down where I come from was

where the ice age went through and left stones." She and her sisters lightened the boredom a little, telling each other stories while they weeded and dug.

Children always find compensations, given half a chance. Near the turn of the century, a child at the Halifax School for the Deaf wrote an essay on his working summers:

Last summer my brother and I reaped the buckwheat all

At least sometimes, the youngest got to stop and sample the products of their labour. WESTERN DEVELOPMENT MUSEUM, SASKATOON/5-H-24

day. After we reaped it next day in the morning after breakfast, my father, my brother, and I cut the bushes until noon, and at 12:00 my mother took a horn and blew in it and my father heard it and he told us to come to dinner. In the afternoon my brother and I cut bark with two axes in the barn. Then I picked the strawberries and ate them in the field and lay before the sun.

And an early Ontario resident recalls the delights of the sugaring-off season:

In the spring we'd make maple syrup. We'd make spiles, and drill a hole in the tree, about thirty or forty trees. From the time I was ten I could do it. You'd get six gallons maybe, and it took about ten gallons to make a gallon of syrup. Before we let it boil into sugar, you'd make candy by spreading it on the nice clean snow. Maple candy, which, of course, you ate right away.

A Nova Scotia boy, growing up in the Annapolis Valley in the 1920s, even enjoyed some of his chores: "We used to have things we thought were fun, but they were work. We had colts, and we helped break those, getting them to go around in circles on a rope. We fed the calves milk from a pail that would have milk and water in it, and a cereal. You'd give the calf your fingers to suck on."

He and his parents both looked for a different future for

Sugaring off was almost a party on farms like this one in Piedmont, Quebec, in the spring of 1902. It took about ten gallons of sap to make a gallon of syrup. MCCORD MUSEUM, NOTMAN ARCHIVES, MONTREAL/MP 029/83(26)

In 1907, Dr. George A. Dickinson wrote a report idealizing the knowledgeable, healthy farm boy in comparison with the poor, sallow city-dweller who rarely saw the sun. His list of the things a farm boy knew might daunt any pale urbanite thinking of taking up the life.

I have in mind a country boy who, at the age of twelve, has passed his entrance and is just entering on his first term at high school. He can do ordinary farm work, as plough, harrow, mow, reap, harness and hitch horses, horse-rake, sow grain, build stacks, load hay, cultivate various crops, milk cows, churn, kill and dress fowl or small animals, feed and care for various domestic animals, prepare ground, sow seed, harvest and store away crops. The sun, moon, stars, clouds, wind and weather conditions engage his attention.

–from *The Country Boy*

him: "Father and Mother were anxious that I get an education, and Father didn't let me do jobs he'd think would be habit forming because he didn't want me to be a farmer. I didn't do the morning chores, for instance. I was the smart one." (Arnold Bent, Belleisle, Nova Scotia)

Apples would keep in cold storage, which was sometimes a pit covered in straw. In a winter farmhouse, their freshness must have seemed a treat. ARCHIVES OF ONTARIO/17038

Both boys and girls worked in the fields—often leaving school to do it—following the rhythm of the year that varied only a little across the country. Whether the main crop was apples or wheat, in May and June the children would help spread manure, dig out stumps and rocks, plant potatoes and turnips, and hoe them. In September and October they would help with the harvest and dig up the vegetables.

On the 24th of May we put in potatoes and Thanksgiving Day we dug them up. We had a big garden, and we kids did it. My sister and I milked five cows morning and evening, and we had to keep the barns clean and feed the pigs, and if things weren't done when Dad came in, he'd be furious and bat us around. In those days, what could a woman do? There was nowhere to turn.

Once I was eleven or twelve, I never spent a full year in school because I had to stay out to seed and to harvest. I could do the harrowing and some ploughing, though not with the biggest plough.

When I was twelve I could hitch a six-horse team as fast or faster than my father. He was very proud of that, and I was ashamed, because I hated the farm.

I was a day-dreamer. The Women's Institute Homemakers' Club had a travelling library, and I used to read everything I could. A lot of it didn't mean a thing, but I knew there was something better. (Nazla Dane, c. 1914, Indian Head, Saskatchewan)

Others, more kindly treated, were proud of their skills, proud of taking their place beside their parents. Margaret Crawford lived on a fruit farm near Chatham, in Ontario's southwestern farm belt. "I was thirteen and a half before my brother was born, and I was my father's right-hand man. My whole family were farmers. I loved the fresh air and seeing things grow, and being out with my family. Everybody helped. I was needed, and I went out. I can't remember being made to go out; everybody did it, and I did, too."

Farm children relax on a hillside. ESTATE OF A.S. MURRAY, P.E.I.

And Clarence Read of Carvil, Ontario, was much happier on the farm than at school: "I only went to school six years. The younger ones stayed a little longer. I hated school; I always figured I could do better at home. I drove teams for the riding plough at first. I wasn't strong enough to handle a walking plough. When I quit school, I did the walking plough, a little crooked at first, but we straightened that out."

Stephen Radcliffe learned the techniques when he was about eleven, breaking new ground on a pioneer farm.

"Now then," my father said, "when the cattle start up, lift on the handles and put the plough in about six inches deep." I did as I was told, but the plough ran to the right. "Press heavy with your right hand," he said. I did so, but the plough jumped out of the ground. The oxen were backed up and another start made. This time the plough went into the beam. "Press hard with both hands," was the order, and the plough jumped out again. After making some more holes in the ground, my father rushed for the house, and did not come back until the field was finished.

The next spring the plough caught on a root while Stephen was struggling with it. "The handles flew up and skinned my breast bone and hit me in the jaw." The work, however, went on, and he broke five acres of land.

Feeding those chickens, Cremona, Alberta. GLENBOW ARCHIVES/NA-1944-1

Harvest was, of course, the busiest time of year. Many stories and memories centre on grain, which was not a Prairie exclusive, but was grown on a small scale on thousands of family farms for home consumption: "We grew wheat, largely for the animals, oats and barley and buckwheat. We took the buckwheat to a flour mill to have it ground for pancakes and muffins."

My dad said he had a lot of eggs in the basket, he had milk cows, beef cattle, pigs and hens, wheat and oats, and potatoes. (Frances Davey, Cobourg, Ontario)

Most children were given time to grow up to the heavier work, beginning by just tagging along with dad, and running errands. "I used to follow Dad around with the plough because I liked the feel of the cool dirt on my bare feet."

Florence Thompson of Black Point, New Brunswick, remembers, "When Dad was out cutting wood, I would go with a lunch for him. Dad would have a kettle on the fire, and throw in the tea, and we would sit there and have a sandwich."

Harvesting was hot, scratchy, sweaty work against time and the weather, but it was also the reward in a good year, which may have been what cast the golden haze over George Bouchard's memory of harvesting in Quebec.

Among the pleasant memories of my early youth are recollections of expeditions into the woods to help my father cut material wherewith to tie sheaves. We sought the stems of hazel trees that grew to the height of a man and to the thickness of the little finger; and when cut I bound them into bundles of about a hundred.

The withes were kept in some cool shady place until harvest time. Does not this practice once more reveal that spirit of economy and foresight that characterized our forefathers?

In *Vieilles Choses Vieilles Gens* (*Silhouettes of the Past in French Canada*) he goes on to describe the harvest as it was done on a small, traditional farm where there was lots of young help available.

A mere stripling, whose little legs scarcely rise above the stubble, distributes withes with the gravity of one accomplishing a task of great importance. When the grandfather, to avoid disturbing the *coupeurs à la faucille* (reapers with sickle, mowers), offers to make the sheaves with the help of the children, it is a sight truly touching to behold. Like satellites the youngsters move about the old man, bringing armful after armful, making up in numbers what they lack in ability, and in eagerness what their hands lack in experience.

There was a celebration at the end of harvest, *la fête de la grosse gerbe* (the feast of the giant sheaf). For this celebration, when work is all finished, several dozen sheaves are heaped up into one huge sheaf...One dances a few steps around the giant sheaf, under the paternal eye of the old landsman,

There were all kinds of chores for children at harvest time—in the fields, in the barn, and, if they were daughters, in the kitchen. PUBLIC ARCHIVES OF PRINCE EDWARD ISLAND, MILLIE GAMBLE COLLECTION/2667/140

before rushing headlong toward the house, now clothed in a festal air to welcome the harvesters.

In the decades around the turn of the twentieth century, new farm equipment was being manufactured to make ploughing, planting, and especially harvesting faster and more efficient. It was part of the new technology destined to transform the nation. Lights flickered on in Montreal harbour in the 1870s. A decade later, Ottawa boasted two hundred telephones, the Parliament buildings were electrified, and the railroad was completed across the country.

Professor William Brow, author of *The Farm Treasury,* an 1883 handbook on farming techniques, was enthusiastic about the effects on the future of Canada and of agriculture.

Our position in the world's main industry is assuming several marked features. In the first place, we are no longer a dismembered country, and unbound by modern highways; the great civilizer of all nations, the railway, has brought the Atlantic and Pacific within six days of each other, so that produce at the foot of the Rocky Mountains can fairly compete with that at Victoria, B. Columbia, at Chicago, Montreal, and at Halifax. Of all revolutions, this is the most wonderful and

Facing page: The children of Gleichen, Alberta, pioneer Walter James combine work and play about 1900. GLENBOW ARCHIVES/NA-2157-1

far-reaching in commercial significance.

Next in importance is the application of machinery. What will follow the self-reaper and binder, imagination can hardly picture . . . the ordinary farmer of Ontario will walk out in the morning and return in the evening of one day, after having cut and bound his fifteen or twenty acres with one man and two horses.

"At harvest time children would be out running errands. They'd take lunch out to the men, or water. Mother used to put oatmeal in the water." (Mary Burton, Vellore, Ontario)

Major farm implement companies had been manufacturing and developing equipment since the early 1800s. By midcentury they were producing a few steam-driven monsters that were the prototypes of equipment that would become more and more sophisticated over the decades. Their Canadian market expanded as the Prairies were transformed into the kind of farmland where the big machines would thrive.

In the meantime, most of the companies' output relied on horsepower, and left plenty for humans to do as well. By the 1870s, though horse-drawn reaper-binders were common, women and children still walked behind them to stook grain, building stacks of eight or ten bound sheaves so they would shed rain. Younger children ran errands and carried lunch and cool drinks to workers in the fields.

The Manitoba Chore Boy said his arms ached and his wrists were scraped by the hay. Nazla Dane's heart also ached when, during the bad years in Saskatchewan, "We'd get five or ten bushels an acre, and I can remember trying to stook grain that was only a few inches high."

Harvest season was the time of year when a small farmer might swap man-hours and equipment with his neighbours, or hire help if he could. He might be a temporary part of one of the crews that came with the steam-driven threshing machines, along with a boss who understood the fearsome belts and boilers. All hands were needed. While the men did the heavy work, quite young children worked with them around the barn in the fog of hot dust that was part of threshing. They would tramp down the straw in the haymow and walk the horses endlessly back and forth, attached to the rope running through pulleys that hauled the hay up into the mow.

When they thrashed, they'd blow straw up into this mow which had a trapdoor at the bottom for letting the straw down. We kids used to have to fill the mow up, tramp the straw down, and I was always scared I was going to fall through that hole.

I used to drive the horse on the hay rope. They would bring the hay in and fill up the fork, and I'd drive the horses out away from the barn to pull the hay up. (Frances Davey, Cobourg, Ontario)

Hay was lifted by a block and tackle to be dropped in the mow. The child driving the horse hooked the cable to the swingletree, drove the horse away from the barn until someone yelled that the forkful was dropped, then turned the horse back to do it all again and again.

There were animal harvests, too, which children were usually kept out of. They had to learn not to be sentimental about animals, though, sometimes the hard way, like the little boy in British Columbia who was patiently trying to tame a wild cat, feeding it, and gradually coaxing it closer. His uncle decided the cat was killing chickens, and the boy was the one who had to shoot it, because he was the one who could get close enough to it.

Even when the children had no part in the butchering, however, they helped to process the carcasses. "We'd kill a heifer in the spring and a pig every fall for the family. I didn't help kill the animals because I didn't like it. You hung the animal in the barn for about a week, cut off what you wanted to use, and salted or preserved the rest to store in the basement." (Ben Goodwin, Cape Sable, Nova Scotia)

Maxine Keith, from an Alberta ranch, recalled: "Branding I was not allowed to see, nor pig killing, though I was allowed to help scrape the pig with a broken table knife after they'd been scalded in that old furnace." Another girl and her sister made a game of stuffing sausages, trying to make them as long as possible.

As Clarence Read remarked, the attitude was mainly matter-of-fact and practical: "You never worried about the animals getting killed; you didn't get too attached to them."

"The first time we saw a colt born it was because Dad didn't expect the foal so soon," Nazla Dane remembers. "We fed the colt milk. Birth and death were there all the time. It's so matter-of-fact. Mother would say we needed three chickens, and you'd go out in

The children were not just along for the ride in Tantallon, Nova Scotia. Children helped guide horses, rake hay, and tramped the hay as it was piled for storage in the barn. PUBLIC ARCHIVES OF NOVA SCOTIA, PANS COLLECTION/N–1782

the barnyard and kill them. It was just part of your life, and you didn't think about it."

Margaret Dixon, also from Saskatchewan, said, "I was there when they butchered a ewe or pigs. Everyone pitched in and helped. It's kind of hard, but it's kind of hard to go hungry, too."

One batch of chickens on a British Columbia farm once got some fun out of life:

My uncle made a cider press, it was a work of art, made out of solid oak. The juice ran into a little trough and into a jar, and the pulp came out in a kind of cake.

He would cut the pulp and throw it into a washtub to put on the compost. I woke up one morning and I thought I was seeing things. There were banty hens flying past my second storey window. They'd appear, flapping and squawking, then drop down and disappear. They'd got into the fermented mash, and they were drunk. (John Rygh, Port Kells, British Columbia)

Because farmers depended on them and didn't routinely kill them for food, horses were sometimes regarded as

Since the boys are all dressed up, they and the calf may have been on their way to a fair in Prince Edward Island about 1920. ESTATE OF A.S. MURRAY, P.E.I.

Ever hopeful, pigs wait for a drink from the pump in the warm summer weather in 1908 in Bondville, Quebec. MCCORD MUSEUM, NOTMAN ARCHIVES, MONTREAL/MP 076/77(146)

helpers and friends and played a major role in the lives of generations of farm children. About the time of World War I, the high water mark, there were more than 3 million horses on Canada's seven hundred thousand farms. Most children learned to ride and drive as a matter of course, when they were very young. They used horses to bring in the cattle, to get to school, and to hitch a ride home at the end of the day. They played games on horseback, just as town kids did on bicycles, racing to school, playing hide-and-seek or cowboys and Indians. Many horses were cherished companions and even considered eccentric personalities. Clifford Hugh Smylie, in a memoir of Thorold, Ontario, wrote that when he was once bitten by a horse, he ran to get a butcher knife to revenge himself, not, he said, because of the bite, but because the horse laughed at him.

Margaret Dixon of Parkman, Saskatchewan, recalls:

I had a horse of my own when I was three, named Dolly. Dolly called the shots; she knew just how far to take me. Then I had Daisy. I had trouble with esses, and the family would tease me: "You're toopid and tubborn, Daithy." I would back her into a barbed-wire fence to make her go. And Dan, an old workhorse; he was just like a barrel.

Farm girls were as much at home with their horses as their brothers were. MULTICULTURAL HERITAGE CENTRE, STONY PLAIN, ALBERTA

given that responsibility. In about grade four, I weighed about forty to sixty pounds, and you could take a fifteen-hundred-pound horse to the forge.

I was driving the horses when I was ten years old. Our workhorses were very quiet, and I loved it. I raked the hay with a horse. That's a very easy operation. You make windrows. On an ideal day you cut it in the morning and bring it in at night. The men could get thirty pounds of hay on the end of a fork.

In the 1940s we had a small Ford Ferguson tractor, and I was driving it when I was about thirteen. (Ruth Lawley, North Sydney, Cape Breton Island, Nova Scotia)

Farm children took on adult responsibilities at an early age, many of them considering it a privilege.

If I was good, and practised my piano, I could take Frank or Nell to the forge to get their feet shod. It was a treat, because I loved horses, and you were big if you were

"After we finished up working with the horses, we'd have to bring them back. If you had a harness to hold onto, you'd be all right. If not, you only had the mane to hold onto. We weren't supposed to ride them in." (Cecilia Murphy, Read, Ontario)

Most horses were gentle, reliable, and always seemed to know where they were going, allowing even the youngest children to think they were in charge: "When I was very young, I used to go with my grandma in the horse and buggy. She'd sleep and I drove the horse. The horse actually drove herself; I just thought I was driving. When I was a little older, I'd stand on the manger and hitch the team to take the milk about two miles for the milk truck to pick up." (Clarence Read, Carvil, Ontario)

My grandfather had me driving a team very young. They were gentle horses; Grandfather had the same team for about twenty years. He had one horse that was afraid of the threshing machine, and Grandfather had made him go close to it to get used to it. I got on him and he ran away, and my grandfather was angry. But a friend said, "You put that child on a horse before she could walk. What are you worrying about?" (Margaret Crawford, Erieau, Ontario)

If horsemanship started gently enough, it got livelier. Nina Grier, who was the child of a ranch near Fort Macleod, Alberta, and a horse enthusiast, wrote:

Buck was my first saddle-horse—I think I was three. I used to ride up to see Roy and Normie, but was afraid to gallop. One night as I was leaving, Sadie gave Buck a cut with a switch and he headed for home on the gallop. For a moment I was frightened, but when I found out how

Boys and ox teams began their work young in Bolton, Quebec, in the 1930s. NATIONAL ARCHIVES OF CANADA/PA 10696

easy it was, and how wonderful, I was thrilled to my toes, and dashed in to you and my mother to tell you all about it.

Roy, Normie, and I would ride old Barney. When he got tired of us, he sat down dog fashion, and we all slid off.

Joe rode to school at West Macleod when I did. I'd see him on Prince a mile away across the alkali. He'd see me, and away we'd go, racing to get to where our roads joined. After a rainstorm we'd gallop up to a mudpuddle on the road and pull up our ponies and they'd slide through the mud.

Margaret Dixon adds, "Each one of us kids had a dependable, safe horse; this was how you travelled. We played cops and robbers on horseback; the one who was dead would have to fall off."

You had to take falls in your stride, and if you were little, you found a fence or a stump to help you climb back up. Sometimes you couldn't: "Once Jinks put his foot in a badger hole and came down with me. When I didn't turn up at school time, they went out to look for me, and there I was in a heap, unconscious. You and mother came for me that night in the buggy." (Nina Grier, Fort Macleod, Alberta)

Farm children say the family's reliable horses really drove themselves.
MADGE BRATHEN, SASKATCHEWAN

Horses did shy and run away, overturn buggies and wagons, and dump their riders. There was exciting advice on how to stop a runaway horse in a 1912 Handbook for Girl Guides, or How Girls Can Help Build the Empire. It was followed by the sensible caution that most girls would be wiser not to try it.

The way to stop a runaway horse is not to run out in front of it and wave your arms (unless you are too light a weight to stop it any other way), but to try to race alongside it, catch hold of the shaft to keep yourself from falling, to seize the reins with the other hand and drag the horse's head round toward you and so turn him until you can bring him up against a wall or a house or otherwise compel him to stop. But of course for a girl with her light weight, this would be very difficult. Her share in such an accident would probably be to look after the people injured by a runaway horse.

Nina Grier's 1940 reminiscence of life on an Alberta ranch is lyrical in its memories of horse and home:

Coming home on a winter night, wagon wheels sounding like water on hot iron, snow crunching under the horses' feet, their breath all steam, icicles hanging from their noses, and the smoke of home going straight up. You taught me to find the North Star. I've seen the Dipper

Could the friendly cow be considering joining the dog as a lap cow?
MULTICULTURAL HERITAGE CENTRE, STONY PLAIN, ALBERTA

from a lot of places, but never as bright or as close as ours.

Going into the stable at night, horses munching contentedly, brushed down, standing knee deep in straw, their eyes shining in the lantern light as they turned their heads, spitting out a mouthful of straw after they had eaten the oats off. Such a lovely, warm, sweet smell.

A farm day ended where it began, in the kitchen, which was

the heart of every farmhouse. If there was a parlour, it was probably kept in cold storage for distinguished visitors such as the clergy, or for Mother's Women's Institute meetings. Casual visitors sat with the family on the back steps on a warm summer evening, or by the fire in the kitchen. Visiting could turn into an adventure.

> Sometimes in the evening Katie and I would go to visit at Jack Hess's. He was very good at story telling, and would end up by telling ghost stories, and then we would be so scared going home on a prairie trail, about three quarters of a mile, with the bushes on the side, with caterpillar webs that looked like heads, and fire flies here and there. We would walk close together, too scared to talk until we got in the yard, then we would run in the house. But we would go again. (Mary Popp, Langenburg, Saskatchewan)

The kids did homework at the kitchen table, or played games, jockeying to get as close to the lamp as possible. Mother, still working, did the mending. Father, when there was time, read the paper, and sometimes read aloud: "In the evening, Dad used to read to us, and he was a real clown and liked to act it out. He read our school books. By the time I

Just thought he'd find out what the sap tasted like straight from the tree. ARCHIVES OF THE UNITED CHURCH OF CANADA, VICTORIA UNIVERSITY, TORONTO

If a calf was hungry enough, it might let you sit on its back. Rimbey, Alberta, c. 1930. ANNE STEWART, ALBERTA

friends gathered round to warble hymns or sentimental favourites that everyone knew, such as "Annie Laurie" and "The Last Rose of Summer."

I played the organ. I walked a couple of miles, paid thirty-five cents an hour for the lessons. My dad liked to sing, and he used to play a little, hymns, like "Take Time to Be Holy." (Grace Arthur, Alnwick Township, Ontario)

"On Sundays, when the relatives would come in, you would gather in the parlour and sing. One of the things that Dad had was a Victrola with His Master's Voice on it, and he was very proud of it." (John Dryden, Brooklin, Ontario)

We sang a lot. Father liked to sing. On stormy days in the winter he would spend the evenings singing, and we would listen. A grand uncle who lived on an island would stay for the winter and sang old songs. A mouth-organ and jew's harp made the music. (Esther McDonell, Enfield County, Nova Scotia)

We did have a nice family life, what with teasing, fighting, playing, later on dancing, practising the newer dances,

was in grade three I was reading grade seven or eight books." (Florence Thompson, Black Point, New Brunswick)

Music was also highly valued. Schools had itinerant music teachers, and children often walked to town clutching their pennies for music lessons so there was someone to thump away at the piano or cottage organ while family and

Passing parade on a farm in Pokeshaw, New Brunswick, in the 1930s, shows the school in the background. Among other things, geese provided feathers for pillows and comforters. PROVINCIAL ARCHIVES OF NEW BRUNSWICK/MND 6/19

two-step, three-step, four-step, French minuet, and also new square dances. We could all play the mouth organ and with some of the brothers small and not enough to make a set for square dancing, we would still practise. Sometimes the hired man, if we had one, would fill in. (Mary Popp, Langenburg, Saskatchewan)

In later years, the mechanical marvels began to arrive, and the voices of entertainers like Harry Lauder wheezed and crackled into the country air. Mary Popp recalls: "Then there was one time our neighbour came over and brought a talking machine with a big horn and round records. Well, that was just the most wonderful machine we had ever seen."

But the home-grown, family entertainment was the cosiest: "On a stormy night Mom would make fudge, and the wind would be blowing. Even the other night when it stormed, I said it was a fudge night." (Florence Thompson, Black Point, New Brunswick)

Then off you went to bed, dressing by the fire and scampering upstairs to a bed warmed by a brick wrapped in flannel, or a pig* full of hot water.

* A "pig" is a pottery bottle.

Women's Work

AN ITEM IN AN 1893 FARMER'S ADVOCATE BEGINS by quoting a fictitious exchange between two farmers on the cost of having an excess of daughters. "'Another girl! I'm goin' to be swamped, sure,' said a farmer recently. 'Yes, there's nothin' like a family of girls and a lot of old horses fer keepin' a man down,' replied the sympathetic neighbour."

The article went on to describe girls as purer and nearer to heaven than boys, and to deplore the fact that "some girls remain in their father's house, though not greatly needed, waiting for some other man to shoulder the burden of their support."

Leaving aside kinder feelings about daughters, few farm girls had the luxury of being a burden. At the least, the girls minded the younger children: "When there was a new baby I was taken to my grandmother's. They'd come and say, 'Have we got a surprise for you!' and I'd say, 'Oh Ma, another one for me to look after.' Looking after the babies, that was the only thing I resented." (Mrs. Arbeau, Grand Falls, Newfoundland)

At the worst, they did their mothers' work. When Nancy Murray's mother died suddenly of pneumonia, Nancy took over her father's household, which included a blind, mute aunt.

I looked after the house from age eleven. It was hard. You'd get up in the morning and think, oh, how am I gonna get through the day.

I didn't like it, for I liked school, but I couldn't go to school and do the work too. I tried it for a month, and the teacher said it wasn't fair to me and it wasn't fair to them.

Mother and daughters follow the mower to rake the hay. PUBLIC ARCHIVES OF PRINCE EDWARD ISLAND, MILLIE GAMBLE COLLECTION/2667/131

Women and girls spent hours getting meals ready; there were few shortcuts from garden or storeroom to the table. PUBLIC ARCHIVES OF NOVA SCOTIA, PANS COLLECTION/N-699

Maud Johnstone, growing up in Bruce County, Ontario, "was the middle one of nine children and by the time the youngest was born the three oldest, who were boys, were away at college or working, so we older girls soon learned the barnyard chores from milking before and after school to hauling feed, haying and thrashing."

When I was thirteen, I had to go to school for about two months, then I was needed at home a lot, to help with the haying and stooking and stacking grain, so my schooling suffered a lot, and I lost interest.

The first year on the new place, we had to herd the cattle in the summer so they wouldn't stray away, and also not get into our grain or other people's until there were fences built. My sister and I would take our lunch, the days seemed very long, and we had no watch to know

She got into town about once a year. "Well, by the time you got the supper dishes washed, the milk pails washed, and the separator washed, it was time to go to bed at 9:00." (Huron County, Ontario Oral History Project)

Girls were in demand both indoors and out. Ethewyn

the time, we would have to go by the sun. Sometimes we would eat our lunch too early, and then get very hungry by the time the sun was low enough to go home. Sometimes we would dig seneca roots, but it took a lot of roots to get one pound of washed, dried seneca roots, which sold at thirty cents a pound.

We all had to work hard, even when small. There were big woodboxes to fill for the cookstove and the heater, which burned big blocks which were hard to carry, ashes to empty. Those were chores we had to do after school. When we got bigger we had to help feed the stock, clean the barns, as the brothers were all younger, the girls had to do outside work, and also help in the house and the garden. (Mary Popp, Langenburg, Saskatchewan)

Mrs. L. Hillis, a widow with a young daughter fourteen years old, found herself at the beginning of harvest with thirty acres of grain to cut and no one to help her do it. In this predicament her little girl proposed that if she was permitted to drive the Pony binder that her mother had just bought, she would undertake to cut the grain herself. The first day's work was entered into with great misgivings, but little Adah Hillis was plucky and stuck right to it day after day until she had harvested the whole thirty acres, her mother meanwhile following the machine and shocking the grain. Mrs. Hillis in telling of her experience after harvest in a letter written to the Deering Harvester Co., Chicago, the manufacturers of the binder, said: "We used it in a very heavy field where our old binder could hardly cut at all, and my little girl ran it herself without anyone giving her any assistance."
–Farmer's Advocate, June 15, 1897

Yokes eased the burden of everlasting trips between house and well. Quebec, 1930s. MCCORD MUSEUM, NOTMAN ARCHIVES, MONTREAL/MP 010/92(23)

The indoor skills they had to learn included making butter, preserving fruit and vegetables and meat, cooking, cleaning and sewing, all with rudimentary equipment. In 1922, a survey by the United Farm Women of Manitoba indicated that although 70 percent of farmhouses had phones, there were few other amenities until electricity became common. A pump in the kitchen was a great boon, the nearest thing to running water most farm women could expect. The survey indicated there were 217 feet to walk between house and well, carrying water to fill buckets, tubs, and kettles. There were coal-oil lamps to trim and clean, fires to light and tend, the ashes to carry out, and dust and dirt to clear up. If you had a few minutes to sit down, you could shell peas, knit socks, do the mending.

Cooking from scratch began with catching the chicken or digging up the potatoes. Knitting began with shearing the sheep and washing the wool. And cleaning started with raw materials such as soda, vinegar, and lye.

Young girls were taught to peel apples and potatoes so the skins came off in a thin, frugal curl; to darn socks without bumps so the wearer wouldn't get blisters; to judge whether the oven heat was "slow" enough to cook a stew or "quick" enough for pastry. They heated irons on the stove and learned the right way to iron a heavy shirt or a dainty Sunday ruffle, and learned, by the flickering evening lights, to mend rugged coveralls or crochet lace.

A rural joke for generations held that you could tell who was boss by the state of the buildings. If the barn was the best available and the house not quite up to par, the man ruled; if the house was the pride of the farm buildings, it was the wife. But whether home was a sod hut or a prosperous brick house, life indoors was busy, and if the women and girls worked with the men in the barnyard and fields, it was a rare man or boy who did any housework, or helped do any women's work at all.

Girls learned to sew clothes and curtains, to do fancy work for decoration, and to mend clothes that had to last a long time. PUBLIC ARCHIVES OF PRINCE EDWARD ISLAND, MILLIE GAMBLE COLLECTION/2667/136

Food production was incessant. The early, substantial breakfast, set up the night before, began the day with porridge made from oats grown on the farm, eggs from farmyard chickens, bacon from a farm-grown pig, bread baked at home, and butter churned from farm milk.

In the Maritimes, where farmers might also be fisher-

It's unlikely the children were this well dressed when they actually helped with the harvest. PUBLIC ARCHIVES OF PRINCE EDWARD ISLAND/3446/HF.70.1778.3.10.2

leave it there all day Saturday, and it was really good at night." (Ben Goodwin, Cape Sable, Nova Scotia)

Everyone remembers farm food with a mouth-watering affection; providing it in abundance was a source of pride for a woman, and being a good cook definitely added to the attractions of a girl of marriageable age. During harvest, or bee time, when threshing crews came or neighbours swapped work, the women and girls produced fifty or more individual meals a day. A typical menu might include "boiled potatoes and turnips, onions and carrots, roast beef, gravy, applesauce, tea biscuits, bread, butter, pickles and home-made ketchup, and two kinds of pie." (Mabel Sanderson, Victoria Square, Ontario) It would have

men, "We had our own chickens to kill, and we ate a lot of lobster in the wintertime. On Sunday we'd have a big pot roast, and every Saturday night we'd have beans. Mother would put them in a big crock with pork and onions and

been a disgrace to run out of food, just as it would have been inhospitable not to offer food to guests who dropped in. And standards were high. Maxine Keith has vivid memories of harvest time in Alberta:

At thrashing time, one farmer had an old-time thrashing machine, an old John Deere that banged and popped. About five or six farmers, neighbours, including my dad, would all take their teams and their hayracks, and help each other. Dad would be away for days, then they'd be at our house for three or four or five days.

My mother was an especially fussy lady, and when it came to our house, she wanted to have lots of food. I'd do the potatoes and haul in the wood and carry the water. It was a lot of work, when I look back and think of it. No facilities, and it hotter'n a bugger.

In 1918, in *Old Days on the Farm*, A.C. Wood wrote:

I don't know that it has ever been poetically observed that in the spring

Mother and daughter show off summer dresses in Alberta during the 1940s. ANNE STEWART, ALBERTA

a small boy's fancy fondly turns to thoughts of rhubarb pie, but I do know that in the fall-time, years ago, on the farm, both the small boys and the old boys had violent hankerings for cider "applesass" and tart pies with "sass" fillin'.

The qualifications of a country girl in days past, considered necessary before she became a bride, were that she could bake bread, make butter, etc., and in some districts a knowledge of making "applesass" properly was deemed important.

"Mom would bake bread pretty near every Monday, and you'd come home from school and it smelled so good."(Inez Anderson, Gladys Ridge, Alberta)

When there were several daughters, as in Mary Burton's home near Woodbridge, Ontario, the kitchen became an assembly line, even in normal weeks. "Mother did a big baking at the end of the week because we often had visitors on Sunday. I did the muffins and the cakes. I'd help out with whatever had to be done."

Mother was allergic to flour, and I could bake cakes when I was five, and I loved it, though I wasn't allowed to put them in the oven. (Ben Goodwin, Cape Sable, Nova Scotia)

The girls did the preparation, apprentice scullery maids

Two sisters and their brother pose with a team of horses about 1920 on their farm near Radisson, Saskatchewan. MADGE BRATHEN, SASKATCHEWAN

morning's ooey, gluey porridge pot and ending with the evening's sticky gravy and pie plates, all scraped and scrubbed clean in water hauled from the well, heated on the stove, and saturated with harsh, lye-laden soap. Soft rainwater was saved for hair and clothes.

About the only things that farm families bought were tea and coffee, sugar, flour, cheese, and, in the Maritimes, molasses. A winter farmhouse was a storehouse of home-grown and store-bought supplies. It was a great temptation to children.

Near Cobourg, Ontario, Grace Arthur said she and her sisters used to sneak into the attic when no one was looking. "We used to have a great big flour bin, put in about three hundred-pound bags of flour. Upstairs in the attic we put a hundred pounds of regular white sugar, a hundred pounds of brown and a big round of cheese, waxed to keep for the winter. The biggest mouse was us. We used to go and pick the lumps out of the brown sugar."

to the family's experienced cook. To make a pumpkin pie, for instance, first you picked the pumpkin; then you peeled it, cooked it, and mashed it. Then, finally, it was ready to be seasoned and go into the pie. Little was wasted in those kitchens. The pumpkin peelings would go into the slop pail and out to the pig pen. Anything burnable went into the stove, though there was virtually no packaging to dispose of. In many households, even the washing water was used again, carried out to the flowers or the vegetable garden.

And there were always the dishes, beginning with the

Picking beans is tedious work, turned over to the girls and younger children in Wellington County, Ontario, about 1920. ARCHIVES OF ONTARIO/17038

Once my mother bought a crate of plums for preserving (weren't her preserved plums good?). You and she went to town, and hid the plums so we wouldn't make ourselves sick. We hunted high and low for them without success.

She told us afterwards you'd put them up under the eaves in the ice house. (Nina Grier, Fort Macleod, Alberta, c. 1940)

Weeks in the fall were spent gathering and organizing the home-grown produce. On Sable Island in Nova Scotia, "We put potatoes in a big bin with a bag over it to keep it from freezing. We put layers of carrots down in the island's fine sand. Eggs were stored in cornmeal. Our well was also in the basement." (Ben Goodwin, Cape Sable, Nova Scotia)

What couldn't be protected was preserved: "We picked berries galore, and Mother canned them and canned meat. When she did that, we were doing the washing and getting the meals." (Margaret Dixon, Parkman, Saskatchewan)

We made butter all summer for the winter, and stored it in crocks in the cellar under the house. We had a churn that you turned the handle on. We churned about ten pounds at a time. Sometimes it didn't take very long, sometimes it took a long time, up to two or three hours. We would take turns. You could feel it break, start to solidify. You wanted to do it—"Can I do it, can I do it?"—to be there when it turned into butter.

You didn't think of it as hard work. It was a routine that was part of life. Really, I think it was about the best time to have been born and brought up. There was always something to do. (Florence Thompson, Black Point, New Brunswick, c. 1930)

The major chores were so time-consuming that women generally organized a weekly schedule, dealing with each one a day at a time, reflecting the old nursery rhyme that begins, "This is the way we wash our clothes, early Monday morning," and runs through the chores for each day of the week—baking and cleaning, sewing and ironing. That was the way the big jobs were handled, along with all the daily necessities. "My mother was a busy woman, I tell you," a sisterless man recalled. "Monday was wash day, Wednesday was bake day, we had baths on Saturday or Sunday. But she really had to do most things most days." (Ben Goodwin, Cape Sable, Nova Scotia)

Hands were brutally assaulted by cleaners that were ecologically sound, but harsh. The 1914 summer issue of *Massey-Harris Illustrated* offered advice on cleaning various items. To clean rust off steel, mix half an ounce of emery powder with one ounce of soap, and rub hard. You could clean tinware with soda and newspaper, and use newspaper to clean lamp chimneys as well. As for floors and other general household cleaning, you used hot water, lye soap, and elbow grease. "My sister and I scrubbed the hardwood kitchen floor with brushes on either side of a bucket with lye and lard and sand to give it grit. And you didn't dare leave a line of dirt." (Esther McDonell, Enfield County, Nova Scotia)

Previous page: This was the way we washed our clothes, with washboards and buckets full of hot water hauled from the well and heated on the stove. PUBLIC ARCHIVES OF PRINCE EDWARD ISLAND/3885/83

About 1900 near Markham, Ontario, Ethelwyn Elliott is making soap while she minds the children playing nearby. MARKHAM MUSEUM AND ARCHIVES/75.92.2

It took hours of cleaning and washing before sheeps' wool got to the spinning stage, ready to be knit or woven. This is 1920s Quebec. MCCORD MUSEUM, NOTMAN ARCHIVES, MONTREAL/MP 010/92(15)

Mother made every stitch we wore, even to starting with sheep's wool and washing it. That's one of the things you did in winter before you went to school, you would help pick the wool, and then she'd spin it into yarn and knit it. Mother was kept busy making socks and sweaters for us all." (Esther McDonell, Enfield County, Nova Scotia)

We had ten or twelve sheep, and sheared them. Anyone who had sheep, spun. You'd wash the wool, pull it apart to get the dirt out of it, and teaze it. The mill carded it. Then you would spin it. You did two balls, twisted them together, then knit nice warm, heavy sweaters. (Florence Thompson, Black Point, New Brunswick, c. 1930)

Girls and women made clothes, mended them, and remade them. "There were four of us sisters, and we each had work to do—made beds, packed lunches, washed clothes.

My mother had been a dressmaker and milliner. We got cast-off clothes from the family, and mother would re-make them. Everybody thought the Dane girls were very well dressed, but it upset Mother. (Nazla Dane, Indian Head, Saskatchewan, c. 1920)

"I learned how to darn socks. They don't bother to do that any more." (Mary Burton, Vellore, Ontario)

Washing the clothes and the blankets and the sheets was one more time-consuming, uncomfortable, heavy job. Water was hauled from the well, heated, as always, on the stove, softened with soda, and then poured into the washtub. Some things had to be boiled to get the dirt loose. To remove fruit spots from cotton, household advice books recommended touching them with cold soap and chloride of lime, then dipping them in cold water. The wash was wrung by hand and hung outdoors to dry or freeze.

Grace Arthur remembers cantankerous early washing-machines that were only a slight improvement.

The first washing-machine I ever saw had a corrugated bottom and a big corrugated plunger. You had to carry the water to fill it. It was work, because you had to carry the plunger forward and back. Then we got a gasoline-powered washer. My sister and I worked it, out in the cold woodshed. My sister fed the clothes into the wringer

and I used to catch them. If you got cloth caught in that wringer, it went round and round until something went bang. (Cobourg, Ontario, c. 1920)

The Saturday night bath ritual wasn't folklore; it was real enough. The more comfortable farmhouses had a pump in the kitchen and some even had a separate bathroom, but there was no turning on of hot and cold water taps. Water had to be heated a container at a time, and the tub had to be filled and emptied.

Any improvements to living conditions were easily re-membered milestones in a family's life:

My sister was born in 1919, and that year we got the bathroom in, and the water tank. Water was pumped out of the well." (Mary Burton, Vellore, Ontario, c. 1920)

But even a pump at the house was better than hauling water from a distant well.

We had a pump at the back door, and a sink in the pantry that drained outside. We had a tank of hot water on the back of the stove, and a wooden tub used for washing clothes. We did our baths in that, too. I scalded my brother Charlie's foot pouring water into the tub. (Anna Murray, Earltown, Nova Scotia, c. 1915)

And Anna very likely helped deal with the resulting burn; young farm girls were trained to a lifetime of nurturing and practical nursing, a necessity when there was little immediate help available to cope with illness and accidents.

Facing page: Water had to be hauled to the house and the barn for drinking, cooking, washing, and cleaning. MULTICULTURAL HERITAGE CENTRE, STONY PLAIN, ALBERTA

Illness and Injury

ACCIDENTS AND ILLNESS WERE A PART OF FARM life and children were prime targets. For one thing, they suffered as a matter of course through illnesses now largely under control in the western world. Measles, mumps, chickenpox, scarlet fever, and whooping cough were taken for granted as a part of childhood, and yet they could all be dangerous. Illnesses now almost forgotten were commonplace several decades into this century. Diphtheria, known as the strangler, struck suddenly and could kill a child in a matter of hours. Cholera, typhoid, smallpox, tuberculosis—the dismal list was long and deadly. And there was very little help for children with chronic mental or physical difficulties either. They were lucky if they weren't hidden, or badly treated:

We had a boy in the school who was mental, and he sat in the very front. Every now and again he'd act up, and the teacher would hit him. We were all terrified of him. (Anne McNamara, Aldershot, Ontario)

I had twin boys begin school in grade one. They were very retarded, but wanted to learn. They learned to read a little by sight, but not to write. When I left the school for two years, they were taken to a specialist who advised the parents to take them out of school, as their mentality was only that of a four-year-old. When I returned the parents asked me to take them back. I thought they would at least have the companionship of the other children, who always treated them kindly. They advanced to third grade reading and simple arithmetic, but were taken out of school again when I left. (Madge Brathen, Saskatchewan, c. 1935)

Memories of farm accidents give the impression that people sometimes failed to take them as seriously as the victims might have liked.

One time a steer got loose when my brother and I were trying to lead him on the end of a long rope, and it dragged me through the bushes. My mother looked me over and said, "It will be all right."

Another time, on Good Friday we always had a ball game at our school to celebrate the coming of spring. Boys, girls, men, and women all played. I was hit by a bat which broke a bone over my eye—drove me down in a buggy to the doctor's office. He put a dressing on and told me I'd be all right. (Arnold Bent, Belleisle, Nova Scotia, c. 1920)

In fact, public health nurse Florence Tomlinson observed: "Doctors were a long way away. People relied on home remedies, and sometimes left it too late. If there was an accident, there was usually somebody around who could help. People developed their own ways of dealing with farm accidents." Most of them had no choice:

Many unorganized districts in Canada have no medical or nursing service. The settlers in these outlying districts often suffer untold hardships for lack of skilled attention. Imagine the hardship of acute pneumonia or appendicitis or brain fever or one of the accidents which are liable to accompany the arrival of a baby, or a fractured skull, arm, or leg, a gunshot wound, or an artery bleeding from an axe wound and no doctor or nurse within twenty or even fifty miles.

—Red Cross, *National Annual Report,* 1921

According to a 1947 Dominion Bureau of Statistics report on nonfatal farm accidents, children under fourteen accounted for 4,700 of 37,200 reported in a year. Farm children were in daily contact with large animals and machinery; they sometimes did physical work beyond their strength; and they

People went to get the doctor for someone who was ill or injured almost as a last resort. If you were driving a sleigh through fresh snow, it could take a long time. PUBLIC ARCHIVES OF NOVA SCOTIA, PANS COLLECTION, W.L. BISHOP 91

were always as careless as most children are. They were burned, injured by machinery, or in half the cases, by falls. They fell through trapdoors, down unprotected stairs, and probably out of trees. They fell off horses and were kicked or

Even with seven children, clothing was manageable in the summer. In winter they sometimes had to stay home because there were no boots or warm coats for them. ARCHIVES OF THE UNITED CHURCH OF CANADA, VICTORIA UNIVERSITY, TORONTO/92.195C

stepped on by them or by other large animals. While many of the burns happened in the house, the great majority of all the rest, understandably, happened in the fields and woodlots. That meant rudimentary first aid, a painful trip back to the house, and maybe into town to see the doctor.

Rural parents were no less caring than their urban counterparts, but there were special problems on the farm, and living conditions that put a constant strain on the immune system. Even comfortable houses were cold, and so were schools: "We had a six-bedroom wooden house, four up and two down. There were stoves in the hall upstairs, in the kitchen, living-room, and parlour. Dad got up at 5:00 and lit the stoves in the hall and in the kitchen." (Florence Thompson, Black Point, New Brunswick)

We used to bank the house every winter, put a crib around the house, and fill it with seaweed. In the spring, we'd put that on the garden. (Ben Goodwin, Cape Sable, Nova Scotia)

Winter clothes weren't as efficient as they are now, especially for children who worked hours outdoors and may have walked or ridden on horseback miles to school, and woolen socks and mittens were chronically damp. "I wore a wool undershirt and pants," recalled Anna Murray of Nova Scotia, "long woolen underwear and then bloomers on top of it. We rolled stockings to get them up over the long underwear. Chilblains were hot and burning and itching, and if you got a blister and scratched, they wouldn't heal for months."

In isolated, crude homes it was difficult to keep warm or clean, or to separate family members from anyone who had a contagious illness. ARCHIVES OF THE UNITED CHURCH OF CANADA, VICTORIA UNIVERSITY, TORONTO

Some families couldn't afford proper clothing. A Saskatchewan teacher remembered a family of children arriving at school in tears one cold January morning; their feet were bare inside rubber boots. A 1924 Ontario Women's Institute annual report noted that some children couldn't even go to school for lack of shoes and clothing, and they used a school relief fund to help as many as they could. Even in less drastic circumstances, clothes were rarely stylish: "My sisters and I wore lumberman's boots in the winter, and coarse boots in the spring. When it got warmer, we'd take our boots and socks off and walk in the cold mud." (Esther McDonell, Enfield County, Nova Scotia)

Preventing illness wasn't easy given the harsh living conditions, lack of refrigeration and effective medications, and poor sanitary arrangements. Children came down with symptoms that would now send parents into a panic:

I had anaemia for almost a school year, and jaundice for several months. They gave me something with iron. My teeth got black, and I hated it, and they brought in a fruit from the West Indies, just for me." (Arnold Bent, Belleisle, Nova Scotia)

The spring of the year I was eleven, I was so run down and thin they all thought I had consumption. Going into a decline, they called it. (Nazla Dane, Indian Head, Saskatchewan)

Children suffered, and sometimes died, of an illness called summer complaint—severe diarrhoea and cramps— probably caused by tainted milk or other food. Kept cool during the summertime in iceboxes and cellars, food spoiled easily, and food-handling was not hygienic. Adelaide Hunter Hoodless founded the Women's Institutes in 1897 to spread health education among rural women after her son died from drinking tainted milk. Mothers were advised to boil milk for at least three minutes, and not to give ice-cream to a child under five, unless it was made at home. Commercial pasteurization was begun about 1917, but it was not compulsory until the late 1930s. General awareness of bacteria and germs, and any widespread understanding of nutrition, was not common among the general population until the 1920s.

"When brother Donald drank the fly water, Mother gave him mustard and water."

In spite of all the hard work, high standards of cleanliness were difficult to maintain; there were flies and mosquitoes everywhere. People fought them off with smudges of green willow and moss, and smeared themselves with oil of citron. They put mosquito-netting over beds and cribs, and had fly drives to swat as many as possible. Children were rewarded with a penny for every ten or twenty flies they killed. Sticky strips of flypaper hung from the ceiling; Wilson's fly pads floated in saucers of water on window-sills, and children were warned not to drink it. But not everyone made the connection between flies and disease. Early public health "clean campaigns" taught mothers that "the fly means filth," and

Well baby clinics were set up in rural schools and villages to give the youngest children a rare general medical checkup. ARCHIVES OF ONTARIO/S15538 RG 10, 30-A-2

people were urged to treat their privies with chloride of lime.

There were periodic epidemics. Rural schools were closed and families quarantined to protect other people. When it was over, authorities would come and fumigate the house with burning sulphur.

My older sister died during the flu epidemic in 1918. I was sent to my mother's old home to be looked after, because

Mobile clinics like this early 1900s version travelled the rural areas with x-ray machines to search for the dreaded "spot on the lungs" that might signal tuberculosis. ARCHIVES OF ONTARIO/S15541 RG 10, 30-A-2

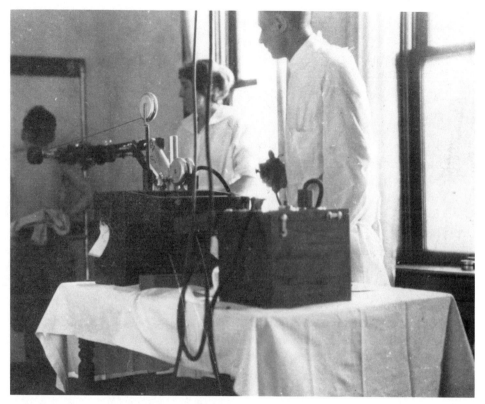

everyone was sick. My grandfather was a very gruff man, and I'd always been afraid of him, but he cut oxen out of wood and made horns out of wire. One of my aunts looked after me. My grandmother went down to help, and she got sick and died. (Arnold Bent, Belleisle, Nova Scotia, c. 1920)

In 1928, we had a winter of bad flu. We had five sick at the same time. The second-oldest girl had peritonitis, and the doctor came after three days. Father made a bed for her in the back of the doctor's car so they could take her into Halifax. When she died, Mother and Father went in on the morning train. She was waked at home, and the church choir sent red carnations. I never wanted to see carnations again. (Esther McDonell, Enfield County, Nova Scotia)

There were many, like a family in Newfoundland in the 1920s, who mourned the deaths of more than one child: "There were eight children, but only five of us most of the time. My oldest sister went blind, and they sent her to Halifax to the blind school. She died at fourteen. Two of the babies died of croup." (Mrs. Arbeau, Grand Falls, Newfoundland)

Children were not always the direct victims.

My mother had t.b.; her sister had died of it in the 1920s. They wanted her to stay in the San, but hers was a mild case, and she knew what to do. She didn't have contact with the rest of the family. We had a hired girl, and mother stayed upstairs with the windows open. I had to talk to her from the hall. I was about five years old, and I didn't understand it. I missed my mom, though Dad made up for it. At night I'd climb into his lap, and he'd read me stories. (Margaret Dixon, Parkman, Saskatchewan)

There was no government funding for health care, and though country doctors were noted for their heroics, getting one could be difficult and expensive, particularly before everyone had a telephone. The 1922 United Farm Women of Manitoba survey found that average distances were five miles to a village, seven to a doctor, and twenty to a hospital.

When they were called in, even doctors had to improvise. Marian Hislop and Ada McLellan, writing about Arcola, Saskatchewan, around 1910, told the following story:

The doctor answered a hurry-up call

to a farmhouse. On arriving, he found that a young boy had swallowed poison. He asked the mother for mustard; there was none in the house. He asked for a couple of other things that would act as an emetic; neither was available; there was no time to spare. The doctor was, on occasion, a user of chewing tobacco. Walking over to the boy he said, "Open your mouth, sonny, and let me look down your throat," and when the lad obediently opened his mouth, the doctor spat a generous portion of tobacco juice down the boy's throat. Up came the poison. Crude? Yes, very; but very, very resourceful. The little boy lived to tell the tale.

In 1916, during the early days of the public health campaign, a doctor speaking to a Women's Institute meeting provided some cold facts, attacked some fallacies, then tried a little humour to make the distinction between casual dirt and the conditions that breed contagion.

Fifty years hence people will say, in a curious reminiscence of the old days, "Do you know our ancestors back in those days had scarlet fever and whooping cough?" We can get rid of these things as our ancestors got rid of nits

---

Rules of the Health Game

Take a warm bath at least once a week.
 Sponging the body with cold water
 each morning is healthful.
Do not eat meat oftener than once a day,
 and eat plenty of fresh fruits and vegetables.
Do not wear shoes with long, narrow toes
 and high heels.
Wear light, porous clothes. Do not wear
 heavy sweaters indoors.
Do not use a drinking cup that others have used.
 –Junior Red Cross, 1922

A Red Cross nurse transports a sick child to one of the organization's outpost hospitals during the 1930S. © CANADIAN RED CROSS, USED WITH PERMISSION

15 percent die, of five-year-olds, 5 percent.

Some people think the only thing they have to do is to put powdered sulphur in their shoes to prevent diseases. But there is another idea that is equally fallacious and yet sounds far more plausible. The idea is that general high health protects against infectious diseases. Because it is so plausible it is one of the worst fallacies we have.

This idea that dirt produces disease has made more trouble for the human race, especially for the women, than anything else. How many conscientious, self-sacrificing women have spent nine-tenths of their lives scrubbing, sweeping, and then doing it all over again, martyrs to the great thought that they were going to prevent disease for their families and other people.

If dirt produced disease, how many boys would grow up to be ten years old? Boys are naturally dirty, and it is a crime against human nature to make a boy wash too often. Girls are naturally clean. I have three

and body lice. The younger the child is that has these diseases, the more sure he is to die. Of the two-year-olds that contract measles, 20 percent die. Of three-year-olds,

boys and two girls, and I know these boys suffered a great deal by being constantly washed. Why should they wash so long as they haven't anything on them that is going to do any harm? Don't fear that they will grow up dirty. When a boy gets to be fourteen years of age, he will automatically turn over and be as clean as he can possibly make himself.

What are dangerous dirts? Not coal dust, mud, or ashes! The invisible stuff that does not show, discharges from our bodies that have disease germs in them are the real danger.

The two great ways in which the new public health affects the homes are these: First, it does away with a whole lot of traditions that wear out people's lives. Second, it turns your attention directly to the real methods by which disease is transferred. (Women's Institute, 1916 *Annual Report*)

Until vaccines and antibiotics were developed and put into use in the 1930s and after World War II, there was little even doctors could do but treat symptoms. They kept patients warm or cool, isolated and quiet, and tried to keep the fever down.

If you had measles you were put in a dark room. My sister nearly died with measles, and one of my brothers had a dreadful time with whooping cough. I don't remember having a doctor upstairs. If you were really sick, you were put downstairs, and if you were downstairs, you had a doctor. (Grace Arthur, Alnwick Township, Ontario)

Florence Tomlinson remembered: "Houses were placarded. Measles was a serious illness. You screened the school, tried to visit homes to talk to parents. Treatment was quiet, fluids to deal with fevers. You kept the room dark. Children got terribly high fevers and bad effects from that. There were deaths from measles in those days."

Baby Hutt Owes His Life to VIROL

I should like to testify to the benefit of VIROL. Our baby boy, when born and up 'till he was one month old, was healthy, then he began to fail; nothing would agree with stomach or bowels. We did everything possible but he kept getting worse, 'till at last we were advised to try VIROL. He was then eight and a half months old and only weighed nine and a quarter pounds; we could scarcely handle him. In ten days we saw a vast improvement, and in three months he sat up alone. He is now eighteen months old, has twelve teeth, weighs thirty-two pounds and never has been sick for one hour since we gave him VIROL. I am sure we owe little Jack's life to VIROL only.

–Mrs. H.S. Hutt

VIROL increases the power of resistance to the germs of diseases and replaces wasted tissue. It is a valuable food in measles, whooping cough, infantile diarrhoea, influenza, etc.

–*The Western Home Monthly*, November 23, 1916

The kids had a good time when the Junior Red Cross director visited Tarnopol School in a spiffy car in 1922 Saskatchewan. © CANADIAN RED CROSS, USED WITH PERMISSION

was quarantined, but otherwise, Mother'd put a mustard plaster on you. You never got too much babying around our place. Dad called you in the morning and if you rolled over and said you were sick, Dad would say, "How do you know you're sick? You're not even out of bed yet." (Clarence Read, Carvil, Ontario)

Mothers treated their families with a mixture of hope, common sense, and home remedies. The mustard plaster was one of the most familiar of these. Badly done, it stung. Well done, it was a warm comfort. The *Farmer's Magazine* ran a recipe in 1919.

Mix one part English mustard with six parts white flour and sufficient warm water to make a thin plaster. Spread

The quarantine period could seem endless to a child:

I remember one summer ruined. I got whooping cough at the end of June and was quarantined for two months. Had to stay home, couldn't go to town, and when we had company, I had to make myself scarce." (Margaret Dixon, Parkman, Saskatchewan)

But unless you had something like spots to prove you were really sick, life went on:

We had smallpox in the early 1920s, and the whole family

this on the centre of a square of old linen and fold over the four corners snugly. Rub the baby's skin with sweet-oil or melted vaseline where you intend to lay the plaster, to prevent blistering.

Apply the plaster, cover with a large, warm cloth, or in the case of a cold on the chest, with a bandage wound around the body. Lift the corner of the plaster from time to time to guard against burning. In ten or fifteen minutes, the skin should be slightly reddened, not scarlet. Remove the plaster, pat the skin dry with soft linen, and cover with old linen.

For a child, the best part of home remedies was probably having Mother make a fuss over you.

The Farmer's Creed

I believe in a permanent agriculture, a soil that shall grow richer rather than poorer from year to year.

I believe in hundred-bushel corn and in fifty-bushel wheat, and I shall not be satisfied with anything less.

I believe that the only good weed is a dead weed, and that a clean farm is as important as a clean conscience.

I believe in the farm boy and in the farm girl, the farmer's best crops and the future's best hope.

I believe in the farm woman, and will do all in my power to make her life easier and happier.

I believe in a country school that prepares for country life, and a country church that teaches its people to love deeply and live honourably.

I believe in community spirit, a pride in home and neighbours, and I will do my part to make my own community the best.

I believe in the farmer, I believe in farm life, I believe in the inspiration of the open country.

I am proud to be a farmer, and I will try earnestly to be worthy of the name.

Frank I. Mann

School

*C*OUNTRY SCHOOLS WERE NOT AT ALL LIKE THE schools in towns. For one thing, everyone who attended was a neighbour, including the teacher. There might be one child in grade three and ten in grade five. There might be any number from five to fifty-five in one school—all ages, all capabilities—tumbled together in one room, and the number could change any time. Children stayed home for a variety of reasons over the course of the year, but on the other hand, if a group of new immigrants arrived in the neighbourhood, the school population might shoot up overnight.

The school might be white painted clapboard, sturdy brick with a bell in a small steeple, or a shack with cold wind coming through the chinks in the winter and flies invading your lunch in warm weather. Inside, the wood-burning stove or furnace would mix its smoky fust with the smell of chalk dust and unvarnished wooden floors, wet mittens, hard-working young bodies, and food. There would be containers of water on a shelf—one for drinking and one for washing.

Out in the yard there would be two outhouses, a wood-pile, and maybe a shelter for the horses. If there was no well, water was imported: "Water was brought to school by the farmer across the road, who acted as janitor. We melted snow for washing hands until spring, then the students carried soft water from a creek beside the school yard." (Madge Brathen, Saskatchewan)

When the teacher gave the signal, the boys marched in one door, the girls in another. In winter the march might continue, round and round the stove to warm up both the air and the children. Then there was a prayer, a chorus of "God Save the King" (or Queen), and the school day began.

While the curriculum was straightforward—reading, writing, arithmetic, science, history and geography, spelling, and occasionally music and art—the timetable was incredibly complicated. The teacher somehow juggled teaching one lesson, hearing another, and supervising desk work, all the while maintaining order and discipline. Older pupils coached the younger ones, and the smart ones finished their work and "listened ahead," moving up the grades at their own pace. They learned by memorization and repetitive recitation, without too much worry about whether they understood everything.

The children competed for class standing and in spelling bees and school fairs. Each small class had its best and worst students, with the rest ranged in order in between. The ferociously fought spelling bees sometimes escalated into

A 1910 Ontario government publication showed the playground at a consolidated school in Guelph, and urged, "Give the girls a chance. At least half of the grounds should be theirs." ARCHIVES OF ONTARIO, "IMPROVEMENT OF SCHOOL GROUNDS #4," P. 16

nine, if their parents thought they had too far to walk. They stayed away if they were needed at home—during seeding and harvest, for example—but the need didn't have to be too great. There were both parents and children who felt that you didn't require much education to be a farmer. As late as 1941, 70 percent of farm children were leaving school at the end of grade eight.

Sometimes bored big boys dropped in for a few weeks in the winter, when things were slow on the farm, ready to harry the teacher a little if they thought they could. Even without the big boys, rural students were pretty good at thinking up ways to shake up the day—gingering up the stove, tipping desks, letting small animals loose indoors.

Clarence Read of Carvil, Ontario, recalls the pranks that kept him and his friends amused:

We had saw-horses and planks for desks, and tipped

matches against other schools with tricky words included in the lists to be memorized from the standard spelling books.

The student body fluctuated. Although there were laws dating from the 1870s requiring children to go to school, attendance was always spotty in rural areas. Children stayed home not only if they were ill, but also if they were disinclined to attend. They might begin school late, at eight or

them over just to break the boredom. One day one of the kids brought in blasting powder used for stumping, and put a hole in the door in the girls' privy and blew a hole in it.

Another day he notes: "The stovepipes in the school fell down today, so that school was dismissed from ten to twelve o'clock." If they didn't fall down on their own, they might be

"In the fall we had to dig potatoes and we did Uncle's too. We didn't mind, because we didn't have to go to school."

given a little help. The stoves were fed things that smelled bad when they burned; a bullet might be popped in, or a covered tin left on top to explode.

Sometimes they didn't bother going to school at all: "We played hookey, just fooled around in the bush. There was a crick run through the school and one day in spring we stripped off to go swimming and someone told the girls there was a lot of suckers in the crick."

The strap was general issue to teachers and principals until the 1960s. Good teachers avoided using it, but thousands of adults remember the sting of it across young hands or bottoms. It was whispered that if you put a hair across your hand, the strap didn't hurt, though experience denied it.

Judging by the expressions, mischief may have been salting lunch for these boys at the Kirby School in 1926 Ontario. Syrup pails were standard lunch buckets for children, and useful for playing catch on the way home. CLARINGTON MUSEUMS/CLARKE MUSEUM AND ARCHIVES, KIRBY, ONTARIO/978.50.4

One exasperated teacher applied it quite impartially: "She just went down the row going swish, swish, on each side." Adding to the strap's effectiveness was the fact that farm parents usually backed the teacher. If you were in trouble at school, there was a good chance you'd be in trouble all over again at home.

Students helped with chores and maintenance at their schools, carrying wood and water, cleaning up. Some teachers used Friday afternoons to replenish the woodpile and generally tidy up for the new week.

After lunch on Friday was wind-down time. On a winter afternoon, when the light was fading, teachers would stand near a window and read aloud to the children. This was when there would be time for small-scale manual training and sewing projects.

> Friday afternoons were special. We had spelling bees, geography matches, and Red Cross meetings once a month. We also square danced, which the children loved. (Madge Brathen, Saskatchewan)

Then the trip home, which was definitely part of the day. If you set a steady pace in the morning, you would get to school on time, but going home, with chores waiting, you dawdled as long as you dared, playing catch with your lunch-pails, maybe racing your horses, checking out a patch of bush, a slough, a creek.

We went three miles to school, and it took us a lot longer to come home, even though it was downhill. You climbed trees, you picked flowers. We crossed a creek and in the spring would count black snakes and garter-snakes. I never learned to swim, which probably worried my parents. (Cecilia Murphy, Read, Ontario)

Occasionally, particularly on the Prairies, children and teachers were storm-stayed, a frightening adventure for everyone in the days before there were telephones to send reassurance to parents.

My sister and I drove six miles to school, an hour's drive in a cutter with a pair of horses. The school had a lean-to shelter for the animals. When lunch-time came, the teacher said, "I think you'd better keep half your lunch, because I think we may have to stay." As the blizzard got worse, we made a chain to the shed and we unharnessed the horses and threw the blankets from the cutters over them, but there was no food for them. And we brought in wood for the fire. It was about three-quarters of a mile to the next farmhouse; well, they made up a great

Facing page: Children, even the little ones, sometimes made the trip to and from school a bit more exciting by racing their horses and ponies. ANNE STEWART, ALBERTA

In 1938, the children's winter clothes look snug, though the car and the house in the background are tired. ANNE STEWART, ALBERTA

dishpan full of sandwiches and hot tea for us.

It was a beautiful sunny day the next day. The bigger boys and girls hitched up the teams. When we drove home I couldn't hold the horses. They were hungry and cold and they cut corners. It's a wonder we weren't killed. I went into the barn and unhitched them, and when I got in the house my hands were so cold they were white and

my mother put them under her arms to warm them.
(Nazla Dane, Indian Head, Saskatchewan)

A teacher recalled a similar experience a few years later.

The morning was so bright and warm I decided to wear a light coat to drive the five miles from my home to school. By 9 A.M. the wind rose to a blizzard.

We resigned ourselves to spend the night at school, when at 3 P.M., two neighbours arrived with a team of horses. We sent the bigger boys to a bachelor's home just across the road from the school. The men carried two little girls across the road to another home. Then the horses were hitched to my car with the remaining nine children and me in it. We were to get one mile to another home.

It was frightening; you could not see the front of the car much less see the road. The men walked on either side of the car, directing me where to steer it. It took one and a half hours to cover that one mile. We will never forget that lady's hospitality, putting up nine children and me for two days while the storm raged, before we were able to walk back to school over ten-foot drifts of snow on the highway. Such a winter. I finally managed to get my car home, but had to walk the five miles to school for several weeks, over high snowdrifts. (Madge Brathen, Saskatchewan)

Until the end of the one-room school system in the 1960s, weather and taxes and crops all affected whether schools were open or closed. They were closed if it was too cold in a small building, or if the community ran out of money to pay taxes or the teacher.

Madge Brathen's first job, beginning in January 1926 at Little Bridge, Saskatchewan, was short-lived:

It was twenty-eight miles from town in a heavy bush homestead district. There were twenty-some pupils, ranging from five years old to seventeen. There had only been six months school in the district, and now I was to have only six months, then their money would run out again. It was closed for two years after that for lack of funds. Grades were impossible, as all were beginners, but so anxious to learn.

Many were, indeed, anxious to learn. As one woman put it, for country children, "school was our outlet," where there were other children, games to play, a chance to match wits, and dress up for the Christmas concert. (Dorothy Shreeve, North Buxton, Ontario)

The lessons people felt it important for children to learn before the 1950s reflect a different Canada, with different values and different work to be done. Stories and poems taught the virtues of honesty and hard work. Even the problems set out in arithmetic lessons presented a sanitized picture of an idealized country of farms. Canada's social and economic ties with Britain were strong, and children were taught British Empire history and British literature, though some of it must have puzzled them.

---

1. What is the least sum of money for which I can purchase either sheep at $6, cows at $28, or horses at $150 a head?
2. What is the least number of bushels of wheat that would make an exact number of full loads for three drays hauling respectively 24, 30, or 36 bushels a load?
3. B sold 76 hens at 73 cents each, 96 turkeys at 324 cents each, and received in payment 24000 cents; how much remains due?
4. A's barn cost 2485 dollars, his house cost 3 times as much, and his farm cost as much as both; what was the cost of the house? what was the cost of the farm?

–*Elementary Arithmetic*, Kirkland & Scott Gage & Company, Educational Series, Toronto, 1882

Those who managed to stay in school until the end of grade eight faced one last test of memory—the school-leaving exam. It was significant for the students because their standings would be published for all to see, and similarly for the teachers, because their jobs could depend on how many students passed.

It was also important for the students who wanted to go on, and for the conscientious teachers who encouraged and coached them beyond grade eight, even though it meant a great deal of extra work.

In 1931 at Wastuna, three students took grade nine by correspondence and one boy took his grade eleven. Their lessons were sent in to the Department for correction. My part was to assist them when they had difficulties.

I was fortunate to spend seven years in each of three schools. In two rural schools I had beginners in grade one then on through grade eight, their only teacher. It was at Phippen that I started seven children in grade one, taking them through to grade eight. They all moved on to high school in Wilkie. It was a proud day when I was invited to their graduation, when each and every one of them had done so well, and one of them was valedictorian. (Madge Brathen, Saskatchewan)

They were the exceptions. High schools were usually miles away in the nearest large town or city, and country students had to board away from home to attend, which was lonely and expensive. Besides, a thirteen- or fourteen-year-old could work like an adult, and there was often pressure for them to simply go to work on the farm. Some children had no choice.

I had one year in high school, then my dad took sick and I had to get home and work. Somebody had to do it. I didn't mind; I was used to the work, and I liked it. (Harold Clarke, Cobourg, Ontario)

Kids like these at Springbank School in Alberta, about 1940, rode horses long distances to rural schools and sheltered them in sheds on the grounds. GLENBOW ARCHIVES/NA-3221-7

There was a lot going on in rural schools besides lessons and pranks. School children have always been a target for groups with good to do or axes to grind, and those in farming areas were no exception. Public health, war work, agricultural improvement—taught largely through the activities of school fairs—and Canadian nationalism were major themes.

The multifaceted campaigns of the Canadian Red Cross mobilized children in schools and classrooms across the country. There were often regular meeting times for Red Cross work and health care talks, and children were encouraged to donate pennies to help other children in need. There were all kinds of projects to aid the war effort during the Second World War, 1939-45, and the organization was an important part of public health efforts.

Provincial Red Cross reports indicate the range of need and the response of school children in the days before health care and social service nets existed.

Newfoundland's Junior Red Cross was new in 1936-37, and had twenty-three thousand members in 681 branches. The children donated enough to the Crippled Children's

Fund to allow a little boy to go to the School for the Deaf in Halifax, and they hoped to help him stay there for several years.

During one year in the forties, Prince Edward Island juniors raised $2,252 for the war fund, provided 4,475 quarts of milk for needy families, and raised $1,255 for a Crippled Children's Fund begun nearly twenty years previously. Some of the money from the junior members would be used in clinics and hospitals maintained by the Red Cross. As early as 1925, for instance, the organization was treating eighty-six youngsters at a clinic for crippled children in Charlottetown, many of whom had never had specialized care before.

The war fund contributions were usually earmarked for relief, such as supplies for orphanages in England, or for equipment such as ambulances and mobile canteens.

Girls knitted socks and mufflers for people in the armed forces; boys made splints; and both packed what were called ditty bags with items such as cigarettes and writing paper. Some of those were destined for prisoner-of-war camps. School children were part of salvage drives, collecting paper, metal, and rubber to be recycled into war supplies. Their gardens became victory gardens, officially encouraged to ease food shortages. Canada's food-rationing system would hardly be noticed by rural children, except, perhaps, that supplies of sugar and dried fruit would shrink.

In 1943, a Junior Red Cross publication carried a letter

During World War II, children collected salvage to be recycled into war materials. These boys in Hudson Bay Junction, Saskatchewan, have lugged nineteen rubbers four miles to school for the salvage drive. © CANADIAN RED CROSS, USED WITH PERMISSION

from the children in Shannon School in Glendower, Saskatchewan, itemizing how they raised a seventy-five-dollar contribution. It sheds a nice light on the skills and tastes in home decoration of the time.

In November we sent you a money order for $75.00. We said we would let you know how we raised this amount.

Early in the fall, during Fretwork and Woodwork period, we began making fretwork articles from wood for a Junior Red Cross Bazaar. This included tables, corner brackets, various toy furniture, bread and meat boards, picture frames, boot jacks, boot racks, paper and magazine holders, teapot holders, hangers, toothbrush holders, teapot stands, pin-trays, book brackets, and pencil holders. Then the sewing included pillowcases, aprons, vanity sets, dresser scarves, oilcloth butterfly curtain tie-backs, cushion covers, magazine holders, crêpe paper dolls, sockees, mitts, pincushions, and other articles. We had a Social Evening on November 13. In addition to auctioning the Bazaar articles, we had a fish pond for the children, and the ladies brought pies for a "shadow pie sale."

Every year we plant potatoes in the school garden and this patch yielded six bushels which sold for $2.40, and we donated this to the Junior Red Cross.

The Red Cross health-care work reinforced the public health campaign begun in the 1880s and 1890s that had taken direct aim at school children. The idea was twofold: to locate and remedy problems, and to educate. Education focussed on sanitation and on teaching people how to reduce infant and child mortality.

A 1920 Manitoba government report recommended the establishment of "a system of rural nursing . . . for the purpose of giving instructions in sanitation and hygiene in the home and the school." Manitoba had four nurses in 1918, and two years later had twenty. By the midforties there were

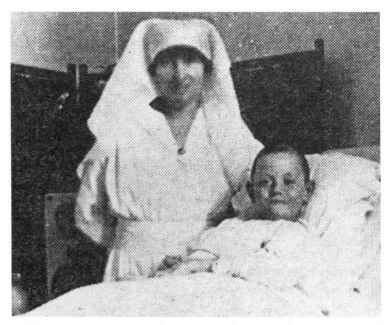

Across Canada, Junior Red Cross members raised money to send crippled children to hospitals where they could get the care they needed. This young patient is at the Grey Nuns' Hospital in Regina in 1922. © CANADIAN RED CROSS, USED WITH PERMISSION

about two thousand of these busy, adventurous women working across Canada. Their reports are full of encounters with balky cars and animals and people as they made their way into some remote and lonely territory.

There was a man near Fort William, Ontario, who refused to buy orange juice for a child with rickets because it was too expensive. Another would not permit his deaf nine-year-old to go to a school for the deaf in Belleville, Ontario.

They were countered by the story of a man who walked six miles through back country carrying his six-year-old to a train to take him to a hospital. When he learned the boy had diphtheria, he left him in the hospital, returned with a public health nurse, and carried other children to his own home so that they could be given the antitoxin.

In the schools, the children looked upon the nurses as friendly visitors who made a school day interesting. They would do their examinations and give a talk on hygiene and hand-washing, the importance of brushing teeth, and how to avoid spreading contagion. In too many small schools, all the children shared one towel and one drinking cup that stood by the communal water container. And any number of people remember being soaked in kerosene to get rid of a headful of lice picked up in school.

The nurses looked for vision and hearing problems, which were widespread and uncorrected. One woman said she didn't know she couldn't see as well as other children until she was almost grown up and went to a silent movie and discovered she couldn't read the subtitles. A man with the same problem recalled, "There were no lights in the school. I had bad eyesight, couldn't see very well. We didn't know what glasses were about, and couldn't afford them anyway." (Ben Goodwin, Cape Sable, Nova Scotia)

All too typically, the nurses' reports listed bad teeth, abnormal tonsils, underweight, goitre, and skin problems, and getting anything done was uphill work, in spite of patches of support. The Red Cross sent out travelling dental clinics. One of them, in Ontario, served 3,615 children in 1936.

A June 1922 issue of *The Red Cross Junior* said fifty-eight out of every hundred school children in Saskatchewan had decaying teeth. The juniors financed two cars, two dentists, and the needed equipment to visit rural schools to treat problems. The tent served as operating room by day and sleeping quarters for the dentist at night. © CANADIAN RED CROSS, USED WITH PERMISSION

In Peace River, British Columbia, the government supplied cod-liver oil, cocoa, and iodine tablets to fight goitre.

The public health campaigns went on until well after World War II. Nurse Florence Tomlinson said,

> In postwar Ontario there was still a need for health units and taking the message to the community. We knew that partly because of conditions doctors had found when they examined people going into the armed forces. The focus was on communicable disease. We lived through seeing those diseases rampant, tuberculosis and polio, and children dying of whooping cough. We saw diphtheria in the early 1940s. Our emphasis was on prevention; immunization was important to us.
>
> We made the rounds of the schools once or twice a year. We used to put a cord across the middle of the room to hang up a curtain and examine the children. Some of the schools didn't have electricity. We took the children into the nearest farmhouse to do vision and hearing tests.
>
> Sometimes, to encourage people to come and hear us talk, we'd take a movie along. The American skating star, Sonia Heinie, was popular then. Some of the kids had never seen a movie.

Farm organizations, particularly the Women's Institutes, did a great deal to support the public health movement.

There was concern about nutrition, and urging from all sides to give children something warm for lunch, especially in the winter. Children carried their lunches from home, but they weren't all as substantial as Frances Davey's: "We'd have a roast beef sandwich, we had it a lot, jam, maybe, and a cookie or two or a piece of cake or pie if Mom had a pie that would carry." Too many had little more than bread and butter.

Some enterprising teachers, with help from a few mothers and women from the WI, made a hot lunch possible, and probably turned young minds from lessons to their tums as wonderful smells wafted around classrooms. Madge Brathen recalls these pleasant memories:

> Lunches were eaten at our desks except in summer, when we would all take our lunch outside in a shady spot. In the winter we had hot soup or cocoa. The children brought milk for the soup and cocoa on Tuesdays and Thursdays. They took turns bringing soup bones generously covered with meat, and cut-up vegetables. The soup was put on before school to cook slowly. The lessons always went well with the smell of this delicious soup permeating through the room in the forenoon.

School buildings and grounds needed attention, too. Although most rural communities looked after their schools as best they could, there were always some that were the despair of school inspectors, who begged authorities to withhold money if they weren't improved. In every inspectorate there were schools that leaked cold air through every crack in the wall, that were unpainted and unwashed, with clogged outhouses that were never cleaned or moved.

We had a white schoolhouse with two lobbies, one for boys, one for girls. Out back were the outhouses. They used to turn them over every Halloween. Maybe that was one way of getting them cleaned up. (Ben Goodwin, Cape Sable, Nova Scotia)

Here, too, lucky schools had the WI coming to the rescue. They supplied first-aid equipment, paper towels, paper cups, and cooking utensils. Zion Line Institute visited the school with the school board during the vacation to see what improvements were needed. They personally helped to clean the school, hired a painter to redecorate it, then put on a social and raised enough money to put in a new stove. Moose Hill furnished dinner for a com-munity bee to clean the school grounds. (Women's Institute *Annual Report,* Ontario Department of Agriculture, 1924)

There was another distraction in the busy life of rural schools—this one a partnership with departments of agriculture and agricultural organizations—and the end product was school fairs. They were competitions, really, in farming and

Health care agencies promoted a hot lunch at school to give the children a nutritional boost. Sometimes produce from the school garden went into the soup. These Junior Red Cross members are in Salmon River, Nova Scotia, in 1925.

Hip Hip Hooray
It's the 24th of May
If we don't have a holiday
We'll all run away!

Baseball on the May 24 sports day in 1930 at Pembarton School, British Columbia. BRITISH COLUMBIA ARCHIVES AND RECORDS SERVICE/C-00924

to make comment on the exhibit, and the rest of the afternoon is given over to sports.

household knowledge and skills, intended to make learning about farming methods and rural issues exciting.

Imagine the excitement at one small school in 1911.

Fair Day certainly proved to be an event. During the morning the exhibits were arranged on tables in the schoolyard, and preparations made for lunch. The judging by some prominent person is too interesting to be wholly ignored, and the group around the judge is sometimes embarrassing. One year the prize money as far as possible was in the form of 25 cent bills. This year, all silver was used, $40 of it in a heap. The judge is asked

The fairs shared ideals and a long, interwoven history with Boys and Girls Clubs, specialty organizations such as swine and potato clubs, and with what eventually became the national 4-H clubs, active all over the country. They were another approach to building an enthusiasm for farming and teaching better ways of working. Organizers, who were generally agricultural activists, hoped the young people would not only absorb the new ideas, but

Facing page: School fairs were important events, and both competitors and visitors dressed up for them in Vellore, Ontario, about 1930. CITY OF VAUGHAN ARCHIVES/MG 1, VOL. 1

would take what they learned home to their parents, some of whom did not take kindly to advice from outsiders on how to run their farms. They also hoped to help immigrant farmers learn how to work effectively in new conditions, and they did, over the years, help to develop and distribute new strains of livestock and seed.

A history of the 4-H clubs in Canada traces its roots to the midnineteenth century, to the days of the Hudson's Bay Company in British Columbia. In 1842, as an element of the company's "teach and preach" policy, Hudson's Bay Chief Factor John McLoughlin directed, "You will let Archibald Spencer's daughter have the loan of a tame cow to milk for herself, and if there is any other girl who can milk, let each of them have a tame cow for herself."

The fairs themselves had their beginnings in 1899, when Dr. James Robertson of the Canada Department of Agriculture appealed to young people as part of a widespread, serious effort to build quality seed supplies in Canada. He offered a reward to farm children for collecting the hundred best heads of grain on their farms and sending them to him. For the next three years, the Robertson-Macdonald Seed Competition was completed by four hundred and fifty kids. It was one of several joint efforts by Robertson and Montreal tobacco baron William Macdonald to benefit rural education and schools.

During the same period, the Maritime provinces were offering bonuses to teachers who would train and then teach

Playing Indian was acceptable, even in a school fair parade. This one was in Saskatchewan in the 1920s.
MADGE BRATHEN, SASKATCHEWAN

what was called rural science. The issue of adding agricultural training to the curriculum of public schools was a hot one for many years. It never made it as a long-term item, but there were school materials produced on the subject, and work based on farm life. And there were school gardens and the fairs.

School gardens were more likely to be co-operative than competitive learning efforts, teaching tools used to demonstrate the value of good farming techniques. They were not entirely successful, partly because rural teachers didn't always know what they were doing, and also because they had built-in problems, for the obvious reason that schools closed for the summer. It was hard to find young people willing and able to tend them, especially as most of them had enough farm work to do at home.

Facing page: The Weaver children pose with a stook at harvest time in Lloydminster, Saskatchewan, about 1920. MCCORD MUSEUM, NOTMAN ARCHIVES, MONTREAL/8556

In 1911, the *Farmer's Advocate* printed a letter from Rainy River, Ontario, that describes how it was supposed to work.

Holidays came near the last of June and we had to find some way of tending the garden. A scholar who was good at weeding and hoeing a garden was chosen to be captain of the school children. When the captain thought the garden needed to be hoed, she would telephone to one of the assistants and he or she got the bunch out to help. When school opened in the fall, there still remained the carrots, potatoes, red beets and grain to be harvested. The carrots and beets were pulled, potatoes dug, grain cut and threshed, by rubbing between the hands and blowing the chaff away. The roots were stored and sold in the spring and the grain was kept for seed. The total amount realized for the sale of produce was fifteen dollars.

The first rural school fair recorded was held in North Dumfries, Waterloo County, Ontario, in 1909, and the movement grew quickly. In 1915, C.F. Bailey, assistant deputy minister of the Ontario Agriculture Department, outlined the philosophy and progress for the delegates at a Women's Institute annual meeting:

During recent years it has been thought that the children should be taught something relating to agriculture, the object being to start them early in life to think along agricultural lines.

This work was begun in the year 1912. In that year we had 25 rural school fairs in Ontario, representing 2,291 schools, or practically half the rural schools in the province. It includes in all 48,386 rural school children. The plots cared for by the children on their home farms, including all kinds of farm crops, amounted to 51,248. We supplied the children with 6,868 settings of eggs of the special bred-to-lay strain. The entries the children made numbered in all 120,000. The total attendance, including children and adults, at these fairs was 150,000. When you bear in mind that this is the result of only three years' work, you will realize how rapidly it has grown.

At first, the fairs amounted to little more than a couple of tables of small displays at the local school, but as the system of fairs and clubs became established, there was a progression for winners from the ribbons and medals and small amounts of cash they won locally, to competitions in township and provincial fairs. Human nature being what it is, high mindedness did not always dictate events. Some youngsters admitted cheerfully that they were in it for the money, like the silver-tongued orator who won prizes speaking on such diverse subjects as Character Building, and Noxious Weeds. "Public speaking was the best paying thing on the prize list; you got $1. Other prizes were 25 cents." (Gordon Bennett, Carlisle, Ontario)

Chances are most of the entrants just enjoyed learning and competing, like John Brush of Essex County, Ontario, a 1927 provincial prizewinner, who wrote enthusiastically: "I close my essay by thanking the Chilean Nitrate Committee for the bag of Nitrate of Soda, for it helped me to have a good garden, win the first prize in my district, and beat Auntie raising cabbages and onions."

For Chilean Nitrate give three cheers!
You can peel my onions without shedding tears.

Sponsors came to include producers like Chilean Nitrate, provincial and federal agriculture ministries, agricultural federations, businesses, and local service clubs, including, of course, the Women's Institutes. The Athens, Ontario, WI reported: "Our interest in the agricultural education of the boys and girls manifested itself in the donation of four medals. These were awarded at the two school fairs held in our district to the boy and girl who won the greatest number of points on the excellence of his or her exhibit."

The prize list grew to dozens of categories over the years, ranging from mounted weed collections to the biggest and best produce and animals, to handicrafts from carpentry to needlework, to displays of canning and baking. There was a perpetual undercurrent of suspicion and some lively and acrimonious debate about who had actually done the prizewinning work, and with good reason: "My dad was handy as a carpenter, and there was an item on the school prize list for a birdhouse. Dad did a fancy one that looked like a stump fence, and I got first prize." (Gordon Bennett, Carlisle, Ontario)

This young boy looks proud of his pumpkin harvest. PUBLIC ARCHIVES OF NOVA SCOTIA, PANS COLLECTION/1941–347

The stern caution that appeared in a 1935 Ontario fair program summed it up politely:

Parents are urged to allow their children to do all the work in preparing their exhibits without assistance. Encourage them in every way, but remember that the work you do for them helps to defeat the object of the School Fair, which is to teach the boys and girls to do things themselves. It is the children's fair; help them to make it a success. Bring your lunch basket and arrange to spend the day with the children.

"The first hot dog I ever had I had at a school fair, about 1923. It was called a Coney Island Red Hot, and cost five cents." (Gordon Bennett, Carlisle, Ontario)

There were, of course, fierce personal rivalries that ultimately became interschool contests, as schools competed by township. "All the schools that entered in the big school fair marched into the fair grounds. You'd bring your pets and calves. The girls competed in baking, flowers, and needlework." Judges were usually local people, and one battle-scarred veteran says parents could be as fierce and competitive as any hockey or little-league parent. "You'd better be on your toes if you were a judge." (Gordon Bennett, Carlisle, Ontario)

As the network of fairs and clubs grew, children could win the chance to travel to larger competitions, where there were bigger prizes and greater glory. Groups of winners from the local and provincial fairs were taken to some of the major farm fairs in Canada and the U.S., often courtesy of the railroads and the fairs. Pearl Bennett, an Ontario winner, who went to Chicago, said these trips added something special to the educational value of the competitions: "It widened your world a little, and they were small worlds."

Competitors wrote essays to describe their activities, and the prizewinning efforts were published. Undoubtedly there were young achievers who had come by their honours honestly, but samples from Ontario Agriculture Department reports do foster some suspicion that the essays had received the helpful attention of a teacher or editor.

Miss Ethel Leach had more than the usual reasons to be pleased with her efforts to grow a home berry patch.

When I entered the Girls' Canning and Gardening Competition in 1915, my principal motive was that sometime I would escape the heartbreaking labour of berry-picking on the hot summer days, over brush piles and stumps in the nearby swamps.

That year, of course, I had to go berrying, and I encountered a wasps' nest and some poison ivy vines, the same day. The result was that I was unable to can any of my vegetables or do any work in my garden for some time.

This year my dreams were realized to a much greater

Members of the Junior Farmers all done up for a historical pageant at the fall fair near Vellore, Ontario, about 1930.
MARY BURTON, ONTARIO

first prize at the fair for her fieldwork, and wrote:

There is quite an amount of work to do in connection with this contest and to win a prize means that the competitor must be industrious. But what is worth winning is worth working for. Besides, there is another reward besides the prize for those who have worked diligently. Isn't it something to be able to pickle, can, and preserve the fruits and vegetables that are raised on the farm? It certainly is. Someday some of the housewives in Canada will look back on their days in the Gardening and Canning Competition and say, "I owe a great deal to those who organized that contest."
–1920 Department of Agriculture Report

A young man from Carleton and Russell Counties, Ontario, winner in the 1917 Boys' Potato Growing Contest, was a more philosophical poet than the Chilean Nitrate enthusiast, and obviously a convinced farmer.

extent than I had ever hoped, as we had enough berries in the garden to do us. The forty plants were sufficient. I have found the work more interesting and encouraging than last year. Experience no doubt accounts for the former, and the weather for the latter.
–1917 Department of Agriculture Report

Miss Agnes Cathcart of Stanley's Corners, Ontario, won

The City folk 'most frown on the farmers
And delight in turning boys down,
They say when we're men we'll see plainly
That we should be living in town.

But I'd kindly like to inform them
That when they want something to eat
They look to the farm to produce it,
Instead of their beautiful street.

Then they find out, much to their sorrow,
That to us they must knuckle down,
And unless we brought them their potatoes,
They never could live in the town.
                    –1917 Department of Agriculture Report

Many school fairs were, like their big brothers, put on hold during World War II, and they began to fade out afterward, or linger as small components of the larger fairs. In 1940, Ontario decided to stop sponsoring the fairs altogether, and agricultural societies stepped in. There were 509 fairs that year, with entries from 107,000 children.

The societies had long been involved in encouraging club work because of the serious purpose behind it. There were early versions of Boys' and Girls' Clubs in 1871 in Cowichan, Saanich, and Chilliwack, British Columbia, with the first official club being formed in Roland, Manitoba, in 1913.

School bags and snappy hats or not, it looks like too nice a day to go to school in Prince Edward Island about 1910. ESTATE OF A.S. MURRAY, P.E.I.

World War I encouraged the growth of the clubs, as farmers everywhere were urged to find ways to increase production for the war effort. The movement became part of that effort, for instance, in the case of the Boys' and Girls' Poultry Clubs started in New Brunswick in 1916. Alberta started pig clubs in 1917, which immediately began to spring up across the country. In this case, patriotism coincided with a changing demand in the marketplace. Great Britain was a major market for Canadian hogs, and when the English discovered a taste for leaner bacon, the clubs helped develop it.

With some funding from government as well as business and the farm organizations, a national Canadian council for the clubs was formed in the 1930s. Finally, in 1952, it became the Canadian Council of 4-H Clubs.

Gordon Bennett of Carlisle, Ontario, was involved with the fairs and clubs for much of his life, first as a farm boy, then as an agricultural representative and deputy minister of the Ontario Department of Agriculture.

My first exposure to Boys' and Girls' Clubs was about 1928 when I was in grade six. A Hamilton service club worked with the local ag rep and bought so many bags of potatoes, good certified seed potatoes. You were given the bag, and you had to return two bags. Eventually you had enough potatoes coming on stream from preferred sources.

HELP THE FIGHTERS TO WIN

SAVE WHEAT—Great Britain and our Allies must have 460,000,000 bushels from Canada and the United States. Normal consumption must be reduced by at least 25% to meet war needs.

SAVE BEEF AND BACON—Normal consumption must be reduced by at least 25% to meet war needs.

The demand for these commodities is imperative. The men in the trenches will go hungry if you fail them. Will you let them fight for you and not fight for them?

YOU CAN USE SUBSTITUTES—such as other meats, fish, eggs, milk, oatmeal, barley, etc., with benefit to health.

YOU BETRAY YOUR COUNTRY'S CAUSE WHEN YOU WASTE FOOD—Over $50,000,000 worth of foodstuffs goes into the garbage waggons of Canada every year. Such waste in wartime is a crime. Your loyalty is measurable by your saving.

EAT PERISHABLE PRODUCTS—Preserve, dry, can, and store the garden truck which has been produced so abundantly this year. By doing so you prevent waste and release storable foods for export.

VICTORY IS DEPENDENT UPON THE EXTENT OF YOUR FOOD SERVICE

October 25, 1917   –W.J. Hanna, Food Controller

When you were drawing in the potatoes in the fall, when you got one that fit specifications, a good show potato, you'd put it under the buffalo robe in the wagon, and store it in newspaper until display time.

As ag reps, we used to try to emphasize that prizes weren't the thing. The competitions made you feel you had some responsibility to make a thing work, and there was a pride of achievement.

With the 4-H clubs, you actually got an agricultural education. You organized in the spring and met once a month. If you had a project, you kept records on it, and at the fall fair there was an achievement day. The main focus was to learn by doing. You didn't get an intensive education, but it created an incentive for the young people to learn more.

The school as melting-pot for immigrant children was another large issue, and one that caused formidable furors in communities from coast to coast. It is the children, in town or country, who are quickest to learn new languages and new ways. And it is the children in school who have daily, nose-to-nose contact with "those others."

Farming communities and their small schools were microcosms of Canada's diversities, with all of the pride, generosity, and potential for conflict that goes with them. Over the years there were storms around the schools—a mix of politics and bureaucracy among the adults, and of bloody noses and bosom friendships among the children.

French-English language issues surfaced as soon as there was a school system. In 1879, French-speaking Nova Scotians in Cheticamp petitioned the legislature for a bonus of twenty dollars a year to hire French-speaking teachers:

> The petition . . . humbly showeth that your petitioners . . . labor under a most serious disadvantage arising out of the impossibility of employing teachers who are both able and willing to impart knowledge in the French language.
>
> A very large number of the youth of this and other counties whose mother tongue is the French one are thus doomed to the cruel alternative, either of absolutely renouncing their right to a fair share in the blessings of a Common School education, or of having recourse to the proverbially difficult task of acquiring knowledge with which they are utterly unacquainted.

Facing page: Members of an Ontario Boys' and Girls' Pig Club promised to feed the pigs they entered in fairs for at least three months prior to the competition, and to exhibit two pigs at a local fair. A 1923 program said the object of the clubs was "to stimulate interest amongst boys and girls in swine production, and to teach them to raise pigs of bacon type AND earn and save money." ONTARIO AGRICULTURAL MUSEUM

Until there were school buses in rural areas, Protestant and Roman Catholic children went to the same schools, and there were sad little rivalries based on religion. Florence Thompson of Black Point, New Brunswick, relates how it took three generations to stop the name-calling.

I went to two rural schools. In one we were all mixed together, and there were never any problems; we never thought of French or English, Protestant or Catholic. The other was predominately English Protestant. We were Irish Catholics, and my brother and I were so afraid to go to school, we would hide and get there at the last minute, and when school was over we would run home. The teachers had a hard time controlling the kids, until finally they got a man who could do that.

My father said it was the same when he went to school there. He had to take a stand, and as my brother and I got older and could fight back, they let us alone. The same thing started when my children went there, only this time, the adults stepped in and stopped it.

When I was older and first working, I lived in a rooming house with people who went to several different churches. We all went our own way on Sundays, and the year my mother died, my landlady helped me get up in time for masses being said for Mom. I didn't know it could be as relaxed as that, and it changed my outlook.

Black children were usually forced into segregated schools even in rural areas, where black families were rare. There was an exception in North Buxton, near Chatham, Ontario, where a small black community was established in 1849, with the help of an antislavery activist. The situation wasn't perfect, but at least it showed that integration could be normal and friendly. One of the black students recalled being treated well in the mixed school she went to as a child, though there were problems in other schools nearby: "When I was going to school, I didn't know what colour people were. We had mostly white children." She later became a teacher in the area and retired, as women did, when she got married. "When World War II came along, a white trustee came and asked me to come and teach in his school. A teacher who had taught me knew they needed someone and said 'go and get Dorothy Shreeve.' His children attended the school and he said if that was good enough for his children, there couldn't be any complaint." (Dorothy Shreeve, North Buxton, Ontario)

In other parts of Ontario and the West, the balance of national, religious, and linguistic backgrounds in a neighbourhood could change overnight when a new group of immigrants arrived. As the Prairies began to fill up with people who seemed exotic to old hands, Canadianization became a major cause. In 1902, J.S. Woodsworth, a founder of the CCF, and a man who worked to better the lot of immigrants, said, "If Canada is to

North Buxton, Ontario, is a farming community formed by black people shortly after the American Civil War. Its school has never been segregated. RALEIGH TOWNSHIP CENTENNIAL MUSEUM, NORTH BUXTON, ONTARIO

become in any real sense a nation, if our people are to become one people, we must have one language. The public school is the most important factor in transforming the foreigners into Canadians."

For a while, in Ontario and Manitoba, children in rural schools were taught in the language of their native country. The trustees were taking advantage of language regulations that had arisen out of the chronic French-English, Roman Catholic-Protestant issues. When the regulations changed during World War I, people who had been encouraged to train and hire teachers to work in their native tongues, found themselves suddenly required to hire English- or French-speaking teachers. The uproar was terrific,

and the anger and confusion it created in some communities must have been difficult for children to cope with.

In the 1940s, activist W.A. Czumer wrote about his own experiences in *Recollections about the Life of the First Ukrainian*

Settlers in Canada. In it he quoted a letter written to a Ukrainian publication that stated the case for Ukrainian-speaking teachers.

> Ukrainians did not protest in the past and do not protest now against the English language. Ukrainians want to know English, and the more the better. Ukrainians would be the first to dismiss from their colony any teacher who was unable to speak English. If they want Ukrainian teachers in their schools, it is only because the best English pedagogue cannot teach anything to a child who cannot understand him and with whom he must converse in sign language.

Czumer goes on to describe a Christmas concert he organized after he was hired to teach in a small school because he could speak four languages. His neighbourhood was delighted. First the children sang "Silent Night" in English, then "Coz to prosze za nowina" ("What News Is This"), led by the Polish children. Ukrainians sang the traditional carol "Boh Predvichny" ("God Eternal"), and finally the German children sang "O Tannenbaum," ("Oh, Christmas Tree"). It was the most unusual Christmas concert ever held in a rural school in western Canada to that time.

The English-born mayor of the nearby village, clearly moved by what is now the norm in multicultural holiday concerts, was overwhelmed:

The curtains were sheets, the costumes home-made, and the Christmas party was a success at the Palling community hall in 1947. BRITISH COLUMBIA ARCHIVES AND RECORDS SERVICE/B-02186

> This evening your children and their teacher had so enchanted me that I forgot where I was. Tears came to my eyes and I had to force myself not to burst out crying . . . I'm ashamed to admit that today is the first time in my life that I've ever heard Galician Christmas carols. Although I didn't understand the words, the aria spoke for itself. I never imagined you had such nice carols.

This effusive response notwithstanding, ignorance of each other's cultures, suspicion, and hostility continued between newcomers and the more established residents. And for everyone—children and parents, teachers, trustees, and inspectors alike—this meeting and mixing was an intimidatingly new experience.

In 1920 *Maclean's* magazine carried two significant articles. The first was written by an anonymous, indignant young teacher describing her experience in a German-speaking western settlement among people she described as being "wished out" of the United States for their beliefs; the elders resisted assimilation on religious as well as social grounds. Under the School Act of the time, she was sent to "replace the German arrangement." Her battle with the elders was not over classes, but over symbols and images, and her emphasis reflects several attitudes that governed the jumble of clashing cultures in many schools at that time. World War I had ended only two years earlier, and unpleasant feelings lingered. In addition, Anglo-Canadians were still very Empire-minded, one more complication for the children to absorb.

When an elder protested that a display of the king's

The girls are wearing pinafores—"pinnies"—to protect their dresses at Sooke School in British Columbia about 1900. The clock and picture of the monarch over the blackboard were in almost every school in Canada. BRITISH COLUMBIA ARCHIVES AND RECORDS SERVICE/24723

portrait and the British and Canadian flags was idolatry, and against the colony's religion, the teacher replied: "It is a Canadian law—school law! I have no wish to interfere with anyone's religious belief . . . but the day I go into the school both portrait and flags go up."

When she went into the classroom one morning to find the king's picture turned to the wall and the flags knocked over, she knew the test had come. "Children," she said, "a very great indignity has been offered to our king . . . I am not going to ask who it was who did so dastardly a thing."

> I was a-tremble with rage. The children were a-tremble with fear . . . Then I asked, "Is there a girl or boy in this school who will act as guardian of their King's picture?" I repeated the question twice over, and then a little girl rose in her place and said, "I will, Tch'r."
>
> Record the name in Canadian archives. It is the name of a little German girl, child of German parents, living in a German colony, surrounded by German prejudices, but constituting herself guardian to her King and Country.
>
> Within a month my thirty little infants were singing "God Save the King" and it warmed my ardour to hear little lisping tongues each day repeat: "We say Gwand old Vlagg."

A few weeks later, *Maclean's* balanced the story with one written by Manitoba's provincial trustee, Ira Stratton, whose job it was to smooth ruffled feathers on both sides of situations like this, and to encourage newcomers to establish and support schools. He painted a sympathetic picture of the difficulties and aspirations of settlers dealing with pioneer conditions and what we would now call culture shock.

A 1925 United Church report on the rural church in the West recommended finding a solution among the children:

> At any rate, the problem, which is now so acute, of the isolated, segregated national group is to be solved and the walls of hostility and suspicion broken down. It must be to the boys and girls that we must look and among them we must work.
>
> The school is one of the most potent agencies of democracy in existence. Not only does it provide for and encourage the freest mingling of classes, but it also enables children of different races to meet on a common ground in those years before the prejudices and preconceptions of their elders have had a chance to forestall their naturally social inclinations.

But these high ideals were difficult to achieve when there was very little guidance for teachers, trustees, or inspectors on how to handle the situations. In 1918, an inspector from New Liskeard, Ontario, wrote:

> There are a number of schools where a considerable part

This 1885 school picture at Kirby, Ontario, gives some idea of what rural children's good clothes looked like. CLARINGTON MUSEUMS/CLARKE MUSEUM AND ARCHIVES, KIRBY, ONTARIO/978.37.1

of the children begin school with no knowledge of English. Teachers are without training, so far as I can find out, to meet such a situation. Working in the dark they sometimes stumble upon methods that are fairly effective, but there is a loss of time and the pupils tend to become discouraged. Could not some means be developed to assist such teachers?

The new children were usually expected to pick up the new language and customs by osmosis, and the children *in situ* were not always welcoming. In a southwestern Ontario community where the "two talks" were Gaelic and English, the kids threw stones at a Gaelic-speaking little boy fresh from a tiny Hebredian island by way of encouraging him to learn English.

Maurice Skwarok met similar schoolyard acclimatizing methods near Keld, Manitoba, and took them philosophically: "I didn't know yes or no in English; we spoke Ukrainian at home. I learned a little bit the hard way; I got beat up by boys who would speak in English, when I didn't know what

The sticks might have been for field hockey or stand-ins for rifles inspired by World War I in this 1916 photo at Pembarton Meadows School, British Columbia. BRITISH COLUMBIA ARCHIVES AND RECORDS SERVICE/C-01059

they were talking about. The teachers were good to me, though. I memorized from a reader and eventually managed to be up near the top of the class."

But while authority ignored the situation, and some kids played rough, kindness and common sense were alive in many schools. In the 1930s, a teacher and inspector in northern Ontario, suddenly presented with a large group of newcomers in a small school, decided to let the curriculum go and teach the children by allowing them to act out everyday situations—playing store and make-believe farming and housekeeping.

Madge Brathen, who taught in several small Saskatchewan schools, recalled:

I had to invent ideas in 1926 to approach subjects for lack of materials, books or paper. The library was like Mother Hubbard's cupboard, bare. We used catalogues to cut out pictures and make stories, as many of the children were not familiar with the English language. Only two English-speaking children in a school of over twenty. The others were German and Mennonite from five years to seventeen years.

And in Beausejour, Manitoba, Frances Raityn said the children around her did learn to get along, even when the adults were fractious: "At school everybody seemed to get along. It didn't matter what language you were, nobody made fun of anyone."

Community Life

COMMUNITY MEANT A VARIETY OF THINGS TO farm families. It was neighbours who swapped work, helped out in an emergency, spoke the same language, or shared a similar background. For the adults, it was the nearest town, where there were supplies and banks and news. There were farm organizations, both men's and women's, that brought companionship, progress, education, and political strength. And church. In addition to their spiritual mission, churches were part of the social and welfare fabric of a rural community.

Churches were often the first communal buildings settlers built and the first they improved when they could, transforming them into sturdy, cherished little centres of wood or stone. They were served by circuit riders who made regular rounds, or by clergy whose responsibilities included three or four small churches. On Sunday morning, the whole family, in best clothes and shiny clean after Saturday night's bath, went to worship, and to visit after the service.

We went to church on Sunday, an absolute must. I would clean all the Sunday shoes. We had Sunday clothes, daily clothes that were school clothes, and changed into our oldest ones when we got home. (Esther McDonell, Enfield County, Nova Scotia)

For families of the plainer faiths, it was almost the only activity allowed on Sunday. They would go home to meals prepared the day before, and to long, quiet Sabbath afternoons.

Church held some perils for children. The services could be terribly, fidgety long, and because such high standards of behaviour were expected, it was easier than usual to get into trouble. Imagine the poor little boy who dropped a bag of hard candies on the open grillwork of a heat vent and had to listen to them rattle loudly down the galvanized pipe into the furnace below. Not only did he suffer loss and humiliation; he would have been filled with the painful awareness of drama yet to come once the family arrived home and Father was able to deal more thoroughly with his embarrassing behaviour in church.

Children also attended Sunday school and Bible classes, where they memorized catechisms and Bible verses, and were rewarded with gold stars and religious pamphlets. They heard temperance lectures and swore off bad habits they hadn't yet developed. A 1900 Methodist Sunday school pledge ran: "I do hereby pledge myself to abstain from the use of all alcoholic liquors as a beverage, from the use of tobacco in any form, from the use of profane language, the reading of bad books and papers, and to earnest efforts to secure the prohibition of the liquor traffic." They listened to stories and occasionally saw magic-lantern pictures of the Holy Land or children in countries where missionaries were operating, then dropped their hard-earned pennies in the collection to help those less fortunate.

> I liked Sunday school because we sang songs. Someone came one Sunday and told us about the poor Armenians who were being killed by the Turks, and in one of the folders was a picture of a small girl. I felt terrible. (Queen Macdonald, Arcola, Saskatchewan, c. 1912)

Not every missionary worked overseas. There were evangelists travelling in Canada, especially in the early years, who would set up camp and hold services for days at a time, drawing people for miles around and cutting across denominational lines because of the colour and excitement they created. In *Experiences of a Backwoods Preacher,* the Reverend Joseph H. Hilts described what happened when some children caught the spirit during a mission in 1887 near Thornbury, Ontario.

> Some little girls, ranging from eight to twelve years of age, went out to pick berries. While thus engaged, one of

them spoke of a sermon she had heard on the previous Sabbath, in which something was said about the conversion of children. They talked on for a while, and then they concluded to hold a prayer-meeting, and ask the Lord to convert them. They gathered into a thicket of shrubbery, and commenced to sing and pray. Before long God heard and answered their simple petitions for conversion, and all of them were blessed and made as happy as they could be.

Some men who were passing by on the road heard the noise and went to see what the children were doing. They found them in a perfect ecstasy of joy and quietly left them without disturbing them. But the story of the children's prayer-meeting soon spread through the village.

Hilts made the children part of his services.

The band of little workers that had received their commission in the berry-field was a great help to me. Everybody wondered at the clearness of their testimony, and the fervour and earnestness of their prayers. For a few days these little ones did a good share of praying for the penitents at the altar.

At the commencement of the third week of our meetings, some of the leading workers said to me: "We shall have to put these children in a corner by themselves, so as to make more room for grown-up people." For two

Church activities were an important part of community life. The Mission Band in O'Leary, Prince Edward Island, about 1910, studied and supported the missionary work of their church. ESTATE OF A.S. MURRAY, P.E.I.

nights this arrangement was adhered to. The meetings were cold, and dull, and dry, and lifeless. Next night I called the little workers back to the altar and all went well.

The established Canadian churches also sent missionaries, not only among Native people, but among newcomers who might acknowledge no adherence at all, or who might be members of other established churches—Greek Catholic or Russian Orthodox. If their attempts at conversion weren't always popular, their practical help and concern for people may have been.

A church worker wrote in a 1930s Canadian Welfare Council magazine:

I can assure you that anything coming into a district from "outside" is a big event. It may be a threshing outfit, it may be a Watkins Remedies van or it may be a big grey-bodied Ford ton truck with "Anglican Sunday School Mission" painted on its sides.

The Sunday Services, often lantern services on the Life of Christ, are wonderfully appreciated by young and old, British and foreign. The small schoolhouse is packed to overflowing. When on tour we make a point of entering the names of any who are specially lonely, specially depressed, or specially hard up. About Christ-

"I come from a lonely homestead in a far distant part of Saskatchewan. If it were not for the visit of the Sunday School Mission Van and for your help in sending me the Sunday School lessons by mail, I would have no Sunday School at all, nor would I have these nice stories to read."

Children raised in the plainer Christian faiths were expected to lead very quiet lives on Sundays. Ethewyn Maud Johnstone of Bruce County, Ontario, wrote:

mas we are able to act Santa Claus by post . . . Christmas cards to parents and children, story magazines and letters have made many a family feel less cut off from friends.

A 1943 *Book of Plays for Junior Girls* published by the Church of England in Canada, includes a character referred to as Girl with Sunday School Paper. Her lines read:

As soon as Grandpa had changed his Sunday clothes and left for the barn, Grandma would say, "Ha' your fling," and we would nearly bring down the house. Grandma would sit at the window and as soon as Grandpa appeared, she would say, "Hold your whist," and we would be sitting like little ladies, asking the 120 questions of the Shorter Catechism when he came into the kitchen.

Normandin, Quebec, was more attractive than many Canadian villages in 1906. For farm families, going to town for church or shopping or business was an interesting break in routine. MCCORD MUSEUM, NOTMAN ARCHIVES, MONTREAL/4044

Those Sundays disappeared slowly in Ontario and the Maritimes.

Church was something to do; you saw your friends at church. But I hated Sunday because I wasn't allowed to do this and that. We weren't allowed to read sectarian things on Sunday. Some very strict Sabbatarians didn't even cook on Sunday. We had to go to Sunday school, and we didn't work on Sunday. (Anna Murray, Earltown, Nova Scotia)

Change came in small ways: "Why, you don't skate on Sunday! I harped, I coaxed until they said all right. The next week my dad cleaned the snow off a little pond so I could skate. My dad went to church twice a day when he was a boy, then Sunday school." (Frances Davey, Cobourg, Ontario)

Some youngsters found innocent ways of dealing with the restrictions: "We always went to Sunday school. Then we'd walk for miles, that was the Sunday afternoon entertainment. Gram didn't always approve of all this Sunday activity, but the young people did it." (Barbara Macdonald, Chatham, Ontario)

If your beliefs permitted, Sunday after church was visiting day: "You didn't do much on Sunday. You went to mass, and cooked your hot dinner when you got home. Sundays in the summer, especially, Mother would invite her sisters and their families." (Cecilia Murphy, Read, Ontario)

There was always food involved, and sometimes the visit turned into a picnic. For some reason, farm people, who live outdoors, remember picnics fondly. Family, friends, the whole neighbourhood went on picnics. Churches and Sunday schools held annual picnics; the school year ended with picnics and sports days. In Newfoundland: "After church and Sunday school, Dad would pick us up in the sleigh, and we'd get under the buffalo robe and go into the bush for a Sunday drive. In the summer we'd have the car-

riage and a picnic, and I would sit up beside him." (Mrs. Arbeau, Grand Falls, Newfoundland) In the Maritimes: "We'd go on a picnic. My mother would make food fit for a king, and we'd go to the Bay shore, the Bay of Fundy, and we kids would pick up pretty shells and rocks to take home." (Arnold Bent, Belleisle, Nova Scotia) In the West: "People meant more to one another; they visited more. We'd have days when we'd take a picnic and you'd go close to the mountains. We had a

No sissy stuff on farm picnics, but chicken and ham, home-made bread and cake, or cookies and fruit.
PUBLIC ARCHIVES OF PRINCE EDWARD ISLAND, MILLIE GAMBLE
COLLECTION/2667/146

great view of the mountains. As a kid I liked the freedom. I liked the freedom, I liked the space." (Inez Anderson, Gladys Ridge, Alberta)

Saturday night social life was more vigorous than Sunday's, but even then, the whole family went.

The young kids went to dances with mother and father at the houses. There was square dancing in two rooms, a couple of rooms that people played cards in; they'd play crokinole and games like that, parcheesi. We were not allowed to play games that looked like gambling, but we played cards. (Arnold Bent, Belleisle, Nova Scotia)

"Whenever my parents went out in the evening, they had to take me with them and put me to bed in some strange place. I quite enjoyed this, as usually there were other children bedded down with me." (May Jackman, Moosonee, Ontario)

The social life was friends who would come and play cards, or Mother and Dad would pack us up and take us to someone else's house. Square dances went on all night, and the kids would be all bundled up and put into bed. (Mary Burton, Vellore, Ontario)

When the dance was at the school, the children snoozed peacefully on the pile of coats at the back of the room.

Anyone who drove a car on country roads in the 1920s had to know how to change a tire because blow-outs were frequent. MADGE BRATHEN, SASKATCHEWAN

"There was hardly a week went by when there wasn't something going on at the hall." (Mary Burton) Then you'd be wakened to go sleepily out for the drive home.

After one particularly bad winter when no one had visited the house for months, I became so shy that in the spring, I hid in a cupboard whenever we had a visitor. (May Jackman, Moosonee, Ontario)

There was more than one kind of isolation to be eased by visiting, as Morris Silbert recalled. His family were dairy

It was hard work, but it was exciting when the threshing crews arrived with their fearsome machines. This photograph was taken about 1910.
CLARINGTON MUSEUMS/CLARKE MUSEUM AND ARCHIVES, KIRBY, ONTARIO/977.11.6

farmers who left Russia in 1905 to escape pogroms. Settling on a farm near Hamilton, Ontario, their loneliness stemmed from being outsiders.

We were very orthodox. We were considered different. You learn to live with it, build up a defence system, so you are better than "they" are. It was a great occasion when visitors came. Because we were the only Jews in the area, we were a depot for travellers.

Even if a visit wasn't social, it was welcome. Pedlars made their rounds, bringing a breath of the outside world with them. For children, the boxes and bags in their wagons were a glittering treasure trove of bolts of cloth, threads and needles, kitchen gadgets and kettles, and even some frivolities such as ribbons, trinkets, and books or games.

Pedlars came around and opened up their wares. Those cases, with all those trays in them with jewelry, threads, thimbles, needles, and sometimes even little knickknacks for us kids, then all the yard goods. If Mother had saved money from the cream cheques, she would buy material . . . or maybe just flannelette for underwear, but we would be happy just to sit on the floor and watch him open those boxes. (Mary Popp, Langenburg, Saskatchewan)

We had one guy who came around with a van, and Mom saved some eggs to trade with him. She'd give me an egg, and I'd get up and get my candy. (Florence Thompson, Black Point, New Brunswick)

Women bartered with the pedlars when they could, just as they did with the storekeepers in town. Cash was saved for necessities and hoarded for the arrival of the Eaton's catalogue, one of the year's big events. The whole family poured over this book of dreams, savouring, planning anxiously how to make the hard-earned cash go farthest. Lucky children got to choose a new dress or a coat, or one toy—perhaps a doll or an air rifle—as a birthday or Christmas present.

The young fry in a rural area had only a few ways to earn money, and in most families, anything they did earn became part of the family income. They might get some cash working for the school, the church, or a neighbour. They might, like their mothers, sell or barter produce and eggs. One child sold seeds, carefully packaged by her mother: "Mother used to grow seeds, parsnip and beets and carrots and lettuce. She sewed up paper bags and put them in. We used to go to the neighbours and sell them for ten cents." (Grace Arthur, Alnwick Township, Ontario)

    Children did a particular kind of barter by selling items advertised in mass-circulation magazines for premiums, rather than for cash. So did city kids, but with the distances involved, it was a lot more work in a farming area. Tim Dickson, who grew up on St. Joseph Island near Sault Ste. Marie, Ontario, recalled:

Get-rich scheme from *The Canadian Boy* magazine, May 1901. METROPOLITAN TORONTO LIBRARY BOARD

How to Get a Bicycle Free !

If you are a smart boy and would like to have a bicycle of your own we can tell you what to do. Send your name and address to the Editor of THE CANADIAN BOY, stating that you wish to get a bicycle. You will receive by return mail ten sample copies of THE CANADIAN BOY. Show these to your friends and get them to subscribe at One Dollar for a year. Secure us seventy-five subscribers and we will give you free a new bicycle all complete, the best in the market. Will you try this? It means some work, but if you are a hustler you can easily take seventy-five orders for this paper. Write to-day, and go to work. If you do not get the full seventy-five, we will allow you our liberal commission to agents on each subscription taken. Hustle, and win for yourself a CANADIAN BOY bicycle. Write us for particulars.

I sold seeds in the spring, and gold-eyed Hormer Warren needles. They advertised in magazines like *Maclean's* and the *Canadian Home Journal*. "Would you like to win a camera? We'll send you a package of seeds which you would be expected to sell in your neighbourhood." I'd plan out a strategy, walking from farm to farm. That's how I got my first camera, a Hawkeye Box 2 Brownie.

There was never much cash circulating among the young in a rural area, so they also sold the magazines for money, and competed for premiums given to the kid who sold the most. "We did everything we could to earn a little money. I sold subscriptions for the *Ladies' Home Journal, Saturday Evening Post, Country Gentleman*. I won a tiny gold pin with a tiny chip diamond, and I lost it." (Nazla Dane, Indian Head, Saskatchewan)

"I hauled water to school, three and a half miles in a buggy, to make a little money."

Alexander Stocki had to face down opposition from an adult to earn his pittance. In the early 1920s, he, his brother, and a friend were caretakers at the large country school they attended.

The floor in the school was very rough, with six-inch spruce lumber, and had to be scrubbed, particularly

On a good day in winter, getting into towns like Port Perry, Ontario, was made easier by the snow that covered and smoothed rough country roads. ARCHIVES OF ONTARIO/6989 S12794

when the weather was bad. We received ten cents for each day at work. This included sweeping that floor daily, dusting, and the furnace had to be started on cold days, but scrubbing that floor was the hardest work.

We had decided to put the floor scrubbing job to Saturdays, which gave us a chance to do the job properly, and since we were paid only once every three months, we asked for ten cents extra for scrubbing floors Saturdays.

I went to a school board meeting with my piece of paper on which I had our time written out, including Saturdays. To my surprise, the chairman got out of his chair saying repeatedly that it was forgery. But the other members did not pull for him, as they thought we deserved those extra ten cents. My legs were trembling from fright, regardless that I was not guilty of any wrong doing.

Prairie children relentlessly pursued gophers and birds for fun and profit.

We made money with gopher tails. We poured water down the hole and hit them when they came up. I always carried a jackknife to cut off tails, just as cold blooded as can be. But they ate things, and if you ride a horse, and your horse goes down in a gopher hole, you just hate those things. We got two cents each for crows' feet. It didn't take long to discover they couldn't tell the difference between crows and magpies. You'd leave them for a while and let them get smelly and they wouldn't want to look at them anyway. They'd tell you to take them away, and you'd wash them off and sell them again to another agent. (Margaret Dixon, Parkman, Saskatchewan)

Sometimes the poor teacher acted as agent; sometimes it was an agriculture officer in town. It has been estimated that in 1921, Saskatchewan children killed 2,019,230 gophers, representing a saving of 1 million bushels of grain.

The Strachans and Dixons are off to Rimbey, Alberta, in the 1920s, probably to share the wagon with a load of supplies on the way home. ANNE STEWART, ALBERTA

Trips to town, though they sometimes included treats and always afforded another opportunity to visit, were never frivolous; there was always business to do, repairs to be made, supplies to buy, mail to pick up. "We drove probably once a week into town for groceries and repairs. When I was a kid and something would break down at harvest time, I'd be kind of pleased because we could get to town."

> "We went to the villages for supplies. You never heard tell of going in just for fun." (Harold Clarke, Cobourg, Ontario)

If there was a farmers' market on Saturday mornings, it was part of the work. Children often "stood" at the family stall selling produce: "When I was ten years old, I started going to the St. Lawrence Market in Toronto every Saturday to sell. We'd leave about 5:00 A.M. My twelve-year-old brother would stay home to mind the farm." (Mabel Sanderson, Victoria Square, Ontario)

I came with Dad when he used to draw hay and barley and pigs down to Front Street to the market. There was very little car traffic, and none in winter; it was all sleigh rides then. I hated Toronto. (Clarence Read, Carvil, Ontario)

> "My grandmother went to market in Chatham from the time she was six. I went on Saturdays, from 7 A.M. to 7 P.M. We stood for years next to a Belgian family." (Margaret Crawford, Erieau, Ontario)

Farmers' day in Clifford, Ontario, was a chance to visit as well as to buy and sell. ARCHIVES OF ONTARIO/2398 S5456

For most rural people, the trip to town was a highlight that every member of the family looked forward to.

The big event of the week was our day trip to town for whatever supplies we needed. There were board sidewalks and hitching posts for horses, and Main Street must have looked like a wild west movie. I used to think that the most exciting sight I had ever seen was the lights of Parkside on a Saturday night—Parkside, with a population of one hundred.

The towns we went to were only villages. They were a couple of stores and a blacksmith's shop. It was a very enclosed world. (May Jackman, Prince Albert, Saskatchewan)

Like the farms, the rural towns and villages changed very slowly. In about 1870, Brooklyn, Nova Scotia, for example, had a gristmill, a sawmill, and a cording mill. Describing the settlement, a local minister wrote enthusiastically, "This flourishing village has recently sprung up. Not many years since there were but two log houses, where now there are a number of fine dwelling houses, a Presbyterian meeting-house and manse, three stores, and a public hall."

Fifty years later, in 1920, despite an increase in population and a few "modern" amenities, the rural world had changed very little. In 1920, Dryden, Ontario, had, apart

from its paper mill, about fifteen hundred people, one sidewalk, gravelled streets, a department store, grocery store, two hardware stores, and a blacksmith's. One of the amusements was to go to the CPR station and watch the trains come in. It was another place to meet, too, to walk up and down and gossip with friends.

For children, if they were lucky, a trip to town included a special treat. They might be given a nickel or a dime to spend on penny candies or, in later days, maybe a movie. "On birthdays, we got up and there was a nickel on our plates, and

Milk was delivered in pails by farmers or collected at farm gates, then delivered by wholesalers to retailers and households. It was not until the 1930s that pasteurization became mandatory. WELLINGTON COUNTY MUSEUM AND ARCHIVES, ONTARIO/PH53 A952.312.25

Grandma, Dad, and the kids off to town in Prince Edward Island about 1910. ESTATE OF A.S. MURRAY, P.E.I.

There were chocolate teddy bears, bull's eyes, jelly babies, thin square taffies wrapped in wax paper. They were good, and they lasted. I liked them better than suckers. (Queen Macdonald, Arcola, Saskatchewan)

Sweet Marie bars cost a nickel at the general store. They were so good, I'd go back and buy another. It was like something out of this world. (George Walker, British Columbia)

But there were snares for the unsophisticated among the tempting possibilities: "When we were small we were taken to town twice a year, once just before Christmas, and once to the races. At Christmas we were given a dollar to spend, I think between us. Once I bought some lovely looking red berries, and was I surprised when I tried to eat them. They were

we knew this dear soul who worked in town, and she would fill up one of those little brown candy bags for us. We thought we were in heaven. (Irma Lowry, Carbon, Alberta)

General stores bartered and sold a wondrous range of things—food, clothes, notions, even candy and toys. This photograph was taken about 1885. CLAR-INGTON MUSEUMS/CLARKE MUSEUM AND ARCHIVES, KIRBY, ONTARIO

cranberries. And they looked so nice." (Nina Grier, Fort Macleod, Alberta)

Farm children seldom got to the nearest major city until they were adults; farm people just didn't travel much. Even if they had the money, they couldn't leave the work or the animals. "You never heard of anyone taking a holiday. I lived about sixty miles from Halifax, and was only there once or twice in my life until I joined the merchant navy." (Ben Goodwin, Cape Sable, Nova Scotia)

We didn't go to town often. Went to Red Deer once in two or three years; it was forty-five miles away. I never went to Calgary or Edmonton until I was almost grown. Nobody ever took a holiday. (Maxine Keith, Rimbey, Alberta)

"I was never on a train but once in my life, and that was Cobourg to Port Hope, about five miles." (Grace Arthur, Alnwick Township, Ontario)

There were occasional special attractions that drew everyone to town and livened up the year, when towns got out the bunting and staged a celebration—Victoria Day, the Orange parade, St. John Baptiste Day, Dominion Day. Elva Jackson, writing about North Sydney, Nova Scotia, said they pulled out all the stops for the sixtieth anniversary of Confederation on July 1 in 1927. There were day-long celebra-

Members of the Junior Farmers near Markham, Ontario, enjoy an outdoor skating party that probably included bonfires and hot chocolate.
MARKHAM TOWNSHIP MUSEUM AND ARCHIVES/987.0.118

tions, a Jubilee message from King George V, and massed school children singing "O Canada" and "The Maple Leaf Forever." The pupils of St. Joseph's School performed *Britannia,* a pageant featuring Britannia greeting her dominions and colonies, and Canada presenting her provinces and their gifts. There was a parade that included school children and the Boy Scouts, plus the town band and a fire-engine with the steam up. The day ended with a bonfire and fireworks on Chapel Hill.

For children in the West, there were rodeos to go to, which ranged from makeshift competitions on someone's ranch to the venerable Calgary Stampede, which began in 1912. The competition was mainly for cowboys, showing their skills, and Anne Stewart of Carbon, Alberta, says "they were sometimes a celebration at the end of roundup or the end of summer, and they might have a barn dance afterward."

Anne says her family "never missed a rodeo or a stampede. We used to leave at four-thirty in the morning—it was a two-and-a-half-hour drive to Calgary—to watch the parade and then go see the rodeo events."

In the 1930s, Irma Lowry, also of Carbon, remembers a neighbour taking everyone into Calgary in the back of a big truck, just to see the stampede parade. They couldn't afford to pay their way into the events, so they would turn around and drive home, stopping to picnic on the way.

And there was, of course, a day at the fair. Occasionally, these events offered little more than an opportunity to visit friends

Walker's World Famous Street Circus
Big Circus Arrives for Celebration

All day long special trains have been arriving over at the CPR, and have been unloading the animals, freaks, insects, and equipment. Dizzy Lizzy, an insane lizard that is quite harmless, has already established herself as a favourite with the several thousand Borderites who spent a pleasant day watching the unloading operations. The dizzy one is 37'7" long and will eat anything and is especially fond of children.

As frequent attempts have been made to steal the trio of German cooties famous the world over for their size and the fact that they have the blood of German royalty in their veins, having been bred on "Little Willie," a special guard is mounted.

–*Border Cities Star*, Windsor, Ontario, November 11, 1919

and neighbours: "The fair was a place to meet. There was not much happening at some of them, but you had different expectations then. You saw other families." (Pearl Bennett, Ontario) But there were also the larger agricultural fairs, where competitions added to the excitement, and there were rodeos, races, and sports, plus the irresistible draw of the midway.

One thing we all looked forward to was the Langenburg sports, and hoped it wouldn't rain. We would all pile into the democrat with our best clothes on and would have new dresses made for the sports and get new hats, real fancy ones.

You paid twenty-five cents for a ride in a car. There was a merry-go-round with music, wire-walkers, horse-races, and races for both children and adults—running, three-legged, fat man's, nail driving, greased pig.

Then the long ride home with the mosquitoes swarming and we had to do the chores and milk the cows, feed the pigs. (Mary Popp, Langenburg, Saskatchewan)

These poor elephants were part of a travelling circus bringing a taste of the exotic to Gravenhurst, Ontario, in about 1910. ARCHIVES OF ONTARIO/2203 S3601

The children were part of it all, entering competitions, marching in parades, getting sick on the rides. "As the school fairs began to peter out, some of the fairs had school entries and junior days. You'd wear costumes, choose a theme, then you'd line up and the judges would go through and look you over. Originally they encouraged you to use all your own material, but then people began buying costumes." (Mary Burton, Vellore, Ontario)

Junior days were part of the big provincial fairs: "We used to go to the Ex in Toronto. There was a special day for Junior Farmers, and they'd have a parade. One year they celebrated an anniversary at the Ex, and we went down dressed in old costumes." (Mary Burton)

Sometimes the children were themselves the competition, as in this 1922 *Toronto Star* description of a better baby contest at the Canadian National Exhibition.

Facing page: Down by the station was an interesting place to be.
PUBLIC ARCHIVES OF PRINCE EDWARD ISLAND, B.H. "JACK" TURNER COLLECTION/2767/16

Lingerie Does Not Count in Baby Show

_____

Wee Ones Are Judged on Scientific Basis Only
Over 400 at C.N.E. FACE FINAL TRIBUNAL
A Tense Moment When Possible
Prize-winners Are Lined Up

"Of course I don't expect my baby to get first prize, but I thought I'd enter him, just to see what happens."

This was the modest and disingenuous statement made by everyone of at least two dozen mothers with whom *The Star* talked yesterday at the baby contest . . .

The judges' decision in a baby contest rests on a scientific rather than a sentimental basis. The baby must be properly proportioned and he must be the right weight and height for his years. If he hasn't these primary qualifications, beguiling eyelashes, curls and dimples, and appealing knots of ribbon on his hand-embroidered dress avail him nothing.

"Lingerie doesn't count," explained an unimpressionable member of the judging committee.

"I'd like to know how much real looks count for in this show," said one father bitterly as he restored his rejected son to his go-cart.

Looks did count, however, as the final line-up went to show. It was a very engaging row of babies that faced the final tribunal. One or two had dropped to sleep and could not be wakened, but for the most part the final runners-up were alert, active, and intensely interested. It was a sporting event of the finest sort.

–*Toronto Star*, September 5, 1922

The Waterhouse children dressed as Red Cross workers for the Chautauqua parade in Cereal, Alberta, in 1929. GLENBOW ARCHIVES/NA-2056-8

A remarkable diversion arrived during the twenties and thirties when Chautauqua set up its tents full of entertainment and uplift. Chautauqua was the thinker's travelling circus, bringing lectures, dramatic productions, magic or puppet shows, and musicians to small towns across Canada and the United States during the summer months. It sent out advance staff who worked with local people to establish a site and sell tickets to highly organized programs that offered something for everyone, including the children.

There was a morning program for kids, including a Chautauqua yell, and an essay competition on topics such as

Facing page: Make-believe multiculturalism was the theme of a pageant at a children's Chautauqua program in Banff. GLENBOW ARCHIVES/NA-841-121

"Why I Like Chautauqua to Come to My Town," or "How I Earned My Chautauqua Dollar." The children performed in pageants, rehearsed and directed by Chautauqua staff, and competed for best costume in parades.

Eagerly anticipated for months, the Chautauqua usually stayed a week at each location, attracting people from miles around and invigorating the entire community. Many rural residents had never seen the like before.

Celebrations, Games, and Other Amusements

RESPONSIBILITIES OR NOT, FARM CHILDREN always found ways to enjoy themselves, as children will, given half a chance. Their surroundings were natural playgrounds. At school there were companions and games; at home there was a special savour to playthings and pleasures, perhaps because they were scarce and spontaneous.

The annual festivals lit the year, some of them important for their religious significance, all of them touched with traditions and memories brought from far away, offering a reason to gather with family and neighbours. For the children they were exciting, though they sound quiet enough now. There were special clothes, special foods and dishes, familiar rituals, and treats.

In the country, Christmas was small wooden churches lit by candles, horses tied outside. "When we would go to midnight mass, Dad always put the bells on the horses, and the moon would be shining." (Florence Thompson, Black Point, New Brunswick) It was the church carol sing, the Sunday school taffy pull, family visits, and the school Christmas concert.

"Ooh, the Christmas concerts," recalled Albertan Maxine Keith, "the best time of year. I was a little ham, I liked to sing alone. I wasn't afraid to do it, though some of the other girls were kind of shy."

Mothers made us dresses of white crêpe paper and tinsel, and we'd have stars. Forty-bloody-below, and we'd do a drill in our crêpe paper dresses. We had an old pump organ at the school, and there was a little English lady who played it. She'd walk through the snow to rehearse with us. She couldn't have weighed ninety-eight pounds, and she'd pump away at that thing, and it'd wheeze.

"I think the teacher had a book from Dennisons on how to make costumes. If you were a rose, Mother would crimp the paper. My sister Audrey was rippling water, with crimped crêpe paper hanging down from her sleeves." (Ruth Hammond, Lister, Ontario)

The school Christmas concert involved everyone—all the children and most of the neighbourhood. The presentation near Cornwall, Ontario, in 1930 was "Mr. and Mrs. Robin

The most important celebration before Christmas was the harvest. Shown here is the Anglican Aurora Trinity Church decorated for a harvest festival in November 1893. Long before Canada's October Thanksgiving Day was established, and even afterward, farm communities gave thanks for the harvest when all the work was finished. DIOCESAN ARCHIVES, ANGLICAN CHURCH OF CANADA

Find a Winter Home," which featured a cast of twenty-five. Rehearsal came to absorb more and more of the school day as the big event drew near. Fathers built a stage at the school, with curtains made of bedsheets, and mothers made costumes and the food for concert night, when everyone turned out, including Santa Claus. In spite of all the preparations, though, there were always surprises: "Another little girl and I were paired because we both had bobbed blond hair. They allowed us to practise looking at the book. When they took it away, neither of us knew the words. It never occurred to us that we had to learn the words." (Anna Murray, Earltown, Nova Scotia)

And there were the superstars.

Our Christmas concerts were another highlight of the year. The students loved to act in plays. I taught tap-dancing, so the pupils added these to the variety of programs. One year, while I was teaching them a square dance, I was playing the piano and calling for the dance, and I noticed a grade one boy who was standing beside the piano, mouthing every word. I stopped and asked him if he thought he could "call." He was very eager to try, and did such a good job that at the concert night he stole the whole show, calling like a veteran and keeping time by stomping his foot. Years later, he had his own dance-band. (Madge Brathen, Saskatchewan)

Zena Kossar said there was magic in her little school in Arran, Saskatchewan:

All of a sudden you would see your school transformed into a kind of theatre. We ordered cloth for costumes from Eaton's catalogue. The angels wore satin and tinsel, and the glitter was so special.

The parents would fill the school up, and you'd get the jitters because you knew Santa was coming. We'd all go home with our rare treats, a Mandarin orange and nuts and a few candies in a little mesh bag.

There was occasional doubt about the concert on the part of parents new to Canada. A teacher working near Blenheim, Ontario, in 1949, said she took an interpreter with her to visit families newly arrived from the Netherlands, to explain that this secular event in no way discounted the religious significance of the holiday. They were used to Sint Klaas and Black Peter appearing with gifts for the children early in December, and to celebrating the approach to Christmas as a purely religious observance. It must have

been a time of very mixed feelings for adults thousands of miles from their roots. But their children happily remember preparations for the feasts, the warmth of visits with families and neighbours, wonderful food, and gifts, though assuredly not on today's lavish scale.

> "At Christmas we went to Mother's brother's. Mother used to cook a goose and put it at our feet to keep us warm." (Grace Arthur, Alnwick Township, Ontario)

Christmas in earlier years meant quiet times and visiting, a much more tranquil time than it has become. "Cloudy, hoarfrost in the morning with gales at night, considerable snow. In the morning I went on snowshoes to Roberts' swamp for greens to decorate the house. Company for dinner, played crokinole." (Unidentified female diarist, Wellington County, Ontario)

With life less complex, pleasures seemed simpler, though no less enjoyable for all that. "Very cold and stormy. The boys went skating this afternoon, and we girls ate apples and drank cider and talked nonsense. Tonight we played quiet games, and David displayed his magic lantern."

Christmas at home began a month or more before the festivities, as children helped their mothers prepare. Raisins had to be stoned, citrus peel cut and candied, and nuts cracked to make the fruit cakes and plum puddings and breads and pies. There were no ready-to-use packages from a supermarket:

> We made mincemeat and Christmas cake and pudding. Christmas Day we'd go to our grandparents'. The girls helped with the Christmas, got the fruit ready. It all had to be picked over and washed and cut up. (Mary Burton, Vellore, Ontario)

Other children helped bring in the trees, fresh and fragrant from the woodlot, and everyone helped to trim them with the decorations they'd laboured over themselves.

We'd go back in our own lot in Nova Scotia and cut the Christmas tree. Decorations were home-made, of tissue paper. We had sparklers and put them on the

Everyone was invited to the Christmas pageant in Ahousat. BRITISH COLUMBIA ARCHIVES AND RECORDS SERVICE/B–02187

tree, and small candles like the ones people use for birthdays. We put them in tin cups that clipped on a tree. You had to be careful of fires. (Arnold Bent, Belleisle, Nova Scotia)

We'd cut down our own tree, made our own decorations. We didn't have too much in the way of gifts. One year I got a little horse and wagon, and so did my twin brother, from Grandfather, I think. (Ben Goodwin, Cape Sable, Nova Scotia)

Mary Popp from Langenburg, Saskatchewan, said the children in her German family "believed the Christ child came during the night and brought the tree and the gifts. The trimmings were paper flowers and chains, popcorn, nuts stuck on the tree with sealing wax. The tree hung from the ceiling, and had candles on it. The presents weren't wrapped, they were hung from the tree. We had red and green sugared cookies and chocolate-covered marshmallow figures."

"Father made three small cutters for us boys, painted them Chinese red with our names in white. When we first took them out, the old sow chased us, and we came running back into the house." (Clifford Hugh Smylie, Thorold, Ontario)

Presents may not have been lavish, but they were nevertheless eagerly awaited by children for whom the lack of money was just a fact of life, made up for by caring: "We had

to accept the way it was. There was nothing to do about it. Dad used to go out and take the heads off two chickens for Christmas. He made us cribs for dolls. Mother made dolls for us out of rags, and a doll for my baby brother out of a work sock." (Irma Lowry, Carbon, Alberta)

"Birthdays were always a cake. Christmas you had your stocking and a great big parcel came from Eaton's. The best doll I liked had a china face and a stuffed body. You took good care. My sister got a cradle that she still has." (Esther McDonell, Enfield County, Nova Scotia)

A little boy whose damaged leg kept him confined to bed was given a buggy whip. With that and his lively imagination, he could drive spirited horses all over Nova Scotia.

Sometimes there was a big surprise, or something meant to be a surprise: "Even oranges were a great treat for us, but I wanted an air rifle one Christmas, and we knew there was one there because it was hidden under the bed." (Arnold Bent, Belleisle, Nova Scotia)

At Christmas we were lucky to get an orange and a few candies, until one Christmas about 1920, when I was six or seven, Mother said, "You better go back and look," and in behind the tree there was a doll and doll carriage. I kept the carriage for years and years, and when our son was quite a chunk of a boy there was a girl visiting, and she put Roy in this carriage, and the wheels just sprawled.

I was so mad at her. At the time it was a calamity. When our daughter got old enough, we got her a nice carriage. (Frances Davey, Cobourg, Ontario)

There were some disappointments: "The last Christmas I was given a doll, the baby doll had come in—to Eaton's catalogue. I was so hoping I'd get one, and I was given another blasted little Lady Eaton's beauty." (Anna Murray, Earltown, Nova Scotia)

The Eaton beauty doll had a china head, eyes that opened and closed, and real hair. The body was kid and must have been indestructible. I was scolded for cutting the eyelashes, and I broke more than one head. You bought new ones. I

A little magic is working at the Ahousat Christmas pageant in 1930s British Columbia. BRITISH COLUMBIA ARCHIVES AND RECORDS SERVICE/B-07045

didn't really like them, they were too much like pretty little girls dressed up in fussy clothes, who couldn't play the way I liked to. (Queen Macdonald, Arcola, Saskatchewan)

One year, when we were about four or five years old, we got china dolls, about six inches tall, with hair painted black. I took my sister's doll and broke it, and my father went to town and got two twelve-inch stuffed dolls with long hair. He said, "Why did Santa leave china dolls for these two little girls?" I remember another Christmas was something different. We got nuts and some candy and an apple and an orange. You didn't see an orange unless you were sick. (Mrs. Arbeau, Grand Falls, Newfoundland)

That little girl also remembered a tradition that is now lost in Canada.

My mother made Christmas cakes, and we'd get mummers. We brought mummers into the kitchen; most of them were teenagers and adults, and they'd play the mouth organ. You had to give them a piece of cake and a glass of syrup; we used to get syrup and water to make a drink. Since we joined Canada, they started with the Halloween, and there's no more mummery.

Across the country, people celebrated Christmas with variations on a similar theme. French Canadian families had a feast after the Christmas Eve midnight mass, and some observed an old New Year's custom, which lasted well into the twentieth century, of asking the blessing of the senior man in the family.

There were thirteen in Grandfather's family, and my father was the oldest boy. We would visit Grandfather's house and stay for New Year's dinner, all his children and their kids, a houseful. Then at a certain time my father would get up and look around and everybody knew what was coming. He would kneel in front of his father and ask for his paternal benediction.

"During my mother's lifetime we observed all the high Jewish holidays. Mine was a real Jewish mama; she loved to cook and bake, especially for the Sabbath. I was the youngest of seven children. Our holidays were always family affairs, and Friday night was Friday night, and everyone came home." (Kitty Fox, Toronto, Ontario)

Zena Kossar was one of the lucky ones, growing up with a happy blend of two Christmases.

We accepted some parts of both holidays. My sister and I, who had learned to harness horses, would go out and harness our favourites. They were called King and Queen, and they were kind to kids. We could barely reach the harness, but we'd get it on and hitch them to

One farm's version of a sled dog in Estevan, Saskatchewan, about 1920. SASKATCHEWAN WESTERN DEVELOPMENT MUSEUM

the sleigh and go out to look for a Christmas tree.

There were nine children in the family, seven boys and the two girls, who helped prepare the traditional food for Ukrainian Christmas celebrations.

Some would be done a month in advance, but we finished between the English Christmas, when school was out, and the Ukrainian Christmas, which falls on January 7. My mother was the captain, and my twin sister and I, when we were eight, nine, ten years old, we did all the go-for jobs.

First came the cleaning of the house. Everything got washed, cupboards, dishes. No work can be done on the holiday. Then came the food. We just loved to get into the kitchen and help. These were special dishes that we didn't do the rest of the year.

My sister and I did the baking of the cookies, about twenty gallon jars of cookies, and the doughnuts. We put them outside in a big box to freeze. We did three braided breads, symbolic of the three Wise Men, and meats and cabbage rolls. The day before we would prepare the boiled wheat for kutia. You add honey and poppy seeds and a few nuts. It's symbolic of abundance.

On Christmas Eve we had twelve meatless dishes. The meat was served the next day, but no cooking was done. On the sixth of January, at about three in the afternoon, Dad would go and bring in an armload of hay, which would be placed under the dinner table, and underneath the embroidered tablecloth, as a symbol of the manger. I just loved the smell of that hay in the house.

As soon as the first star appeared in the north, the whole family would sit down to this special supper. The windows were usually covered in frost, and my sister and I would melt little holes in it with our fingers, to try to see the star, because we fasted all day, and we were starved. (Zena Kossar, Arran, Saskatchewan)

If weather permitted, family, friends, and neighbours went carolling. If a priest was available, there was a community church service. If not, observances were held at home. By the late 1930s, they could listen to Ukrainian carols on the radio.

In 1936, the CBC broadcast a nationwide program called "Canada Celebrates Christmas," a wonder at the time, and a portent of Christmases to come. It began by linking greetings from King George VI in England with messages from the other countries of the Commonwealth. Then from across Canada it brought in voices and sounds that included a signalman watching over ships from a tower high above Halifax harbour; a transcontinental train pulling into Field, British Columbia; a golf foursome in Victoria (the contact of the driver with the ball could be distinctly heard); a simple Christmas service in Prince Albert, Saskatchewan; and a plane landing at Edmonton with mail from the Arctic.

It synchronized choirs from nine cities, each singing a line or two from carols. The New Glasgow *Chronicle*, full of praise, described the finish of this truly astounding effort: "The message from (the Governor-General) His Excellency Lord Tweedsmuir, then from the children at different points clear across Canada, came the cutest and dearest greetings." The global village was taking shape.

When the glow of holidays darkened into winter, there was a little leisure time for children, and the winter countryside to play in. There were toboggans, snowshoes, bobsleds, and outdoor skating rinks laboriously scraped clear of snow, where small children learned to skate on double-bladed bob skates, holding onto the back of a chair. "We used to have a big long sleigh, and we used to all go to English Church hill. Someone would get on the small one and hook their feet over the big one, and down the hill you'd go." (Grace Arthur, Alnwick Township, Ontario)

My father made me a bobsled, and I was very popular with my bobsled. I'd say you could ride down in it, if

Staying on top of the snow in Kildonan Park, Manitoba, in 1916.
PROVINCIAL ARCHIVES OF MANITOBA, MARTHA KNAPP COLLECTION 66/N17398

you'd pull it back up. When I was a little older, we had a big dog, and he had a harness. My dad made a sled with two little holes on the front runners, and we'd harness the dog and go into the bush, my girlfriend and I, and take beans and bacon and camp coffee that you made with boiled water. (Mrs. Arbeau, Grand Falls, Newfoundland)

Skating and hockey were popular winter activities, though equipment and conditions were rarely perfect.

We had a big pond right across the road from our house where we'd go skating, and have sleigh-riding parties. Our house was used to come in and get warm. My mother would have hot chocolate ready for us. (Nancy Semple, Three Rivers, Quebec)

We had mud flats near us in B.C. and maybe twice a winter we got a freeze. We'd have a twenty-acre field of sheer ice. You could skate ten miles, easy. The only thing we'd have to worry about was the fences. (John Rygh, Port Kells, British Columbia)

We had a lake on our place; my brother's friends would clean the snow off and we'd skate and play hockey. I played hockey with the boys. We had skates and a stick, no pads. I never owned a pair of new skates. (Maxine Keith, Rimbey, Alberta)

A home-made sled and a frozen pond were all you needed for winter fun, as long as the chores were finished first. ESTATE OF A.S. MURRAY, P.E.I.

made shin-pads of magazines or catalogues. Hockey sticks might be cut from the nearest tree, and a slice of wood or what was politely termed a road apple could serve as a puck.

Easter was a religious observance, without the chocolate overtones it has taken on. Its association with the brightening arrival of spring, however, made it an appropriate time for the girls and women to dress up for church. Hats, which have disappeared from most women's wardrobes, were important, and at Easter, if a woman could not afford new clothes for herself and her daughters, she could put new ribbons and flowers on their hats to make them almost as good as new.

Nobody had skates that fit them; they were hand-me-downs. Nobody thought anything about it, it was the norm. When you skated you froze your feet and you knew it would happen. It hurts. First it's absolutely numb, no feeling, then when you start to feel it, it tingles, then it starts to hurt, and you scream and jump around. (Jack Sutherland, Moose Jaw, Saskatchewan)

Any other hockey equipment was improvised. The effete

There were family gatherings and traditional ham dinners, and occasionally an egg hunt. Esther McDonell, in Enfield County, Nova Scotia, has a warm family memory: "Easter was always a special day, apart from church. My brother Ernest would get lovely hemlock boughs, and get moss. We had the house banked for warmth, and there'd be

Children a long way from elaborate playgrounds find a way to create some fun out of available materials.
ARCHIVES OF THE UNITED CHURCH OF CANADA, VICTORIA UNIVERSITY, TORONTO/92.195C

moss. He'd line the boughs with moss to make a nest for each child for painted eggs and jelly beans."

Anne Stewart, in Carbon, Alberta, remembers when she and a young uncle were in disgrace because of some horseplay: "My uncle and I were colouring eggs one year, and he slipped a raw one in. We were throwing them back and forth, and I saw him pick that one up, and I ducked and it hit my grandmother's sewing machine and we were both in trouble. We left."

In earlier days, there was no such wicked waste. Maxine Keith of Rimbey, Alberta, recalls colouring eggs with home-made dyes of boiled onion skins or beets. "Then I always knew for sure what I was going to have for breakfast the day after Easter, a hard boiled egg."

Self-reliant in so many ways, farm children were self-reliant when it came to amusement, too. There was no closet full of toys. Except when the family had visitors, their playmates were their brothers and sisters, animals, their own imaginations, and the farm. They could hunt or fish or build forts, paddle in sloughs or ponds, ride horses, or play games such as hide-and-seek in the barn. Ruth Lawley, a North Sydney, Cape Breton Island, girl says her safety-minded father wouldn't keep a bull partly so that his children could enjoy the barn: "Father was extremely cautious, foreseeing problems. He wouldn't keep a bull because, he told us later, 'you kids enjoyed the barn and enjoyed the cattle, and I didn't want problems.'"

We played in the hayloft, just bouncing around, or we played standard games like hide-and-seek. You always hid in the same places. In the barn was a good place because you could get in and cover yourself with hay. A lot of it was play-acting, pretending you didn't know where anyone was hiding. We'd go fishing around the spring. Nobody minded you fishing on their property. (Arnold Bent, Belleisle, Nova Scotia)

A pond offered endless possibilities for curious youngsters.

There was a pond near us, at the edge of the wood. You'd see beaver, and big blue herons, and that's where we played. We could swim in the pond. My brother and I would hike out into the woods and build little forts. School was kind of a relief, because there were other kids. (Tim Dickson, St. Joseph Island, Ontario)

Imagination and the natural world made up for a lack of material possessions. A hollyhock blossom became a

Fishing didn't always bring in enough for dinner, but it was a good way to spend a little time in the summer. PUBLIC ARCHIVES OF PRINCE EDWARD ISLAND, MILLIE GAMBLE COLLECTION/2667/126

If you were a boy, and you wanted to go swimming, says one farmer, you just stripped off and jumped in, like these athletes at the Hillsborough River near Charlottetown, Prince Edward Island. PUBLIC ARCHIVES OF PRINCE EDWARD ISLAND, B.H. "JACK" TURNER COLLECTION/2767/21

ballet dancer. You could tell a story with a bleeding heart, stick a maple key on your nose, make a hideous screeching noise with a blade of grass, play conkers with a chestnut on a string.

In Alberta, Inez Anderson

played mud pies, we made tree houses. You learned to amuse yourself. Being an only child, I got pleasure out of being around other children, and when I was alone, I'd pretend lots. I used to talk to myself, and play school. I did have a bike, and you'd think your bike was a car. I can remember Dad buying a licence for a radio. We listened to Don Messer, and Mom and Dad would dance with us.

Her father made a make-believe gearshift for her wagon.

Her mother made her a hammock out of gunny sacks, binder twine, and a couple of stray boards. An old shed became a playhouse, scrubbed and furnished with a scrap of carpet and a discarded table and chair.

Farm children kept an array of pets. Inez Anderson had a cat that actually let her dress it in doll's clothes and push it

Most cats and dogs had their own work to do on family farms, but some of them lived happily as pets for the children. ESTATE OF A.S. MURRAY, P.E.I.

around in a buggy. Margaret Dixon, from Saskatchewan, said, "Mom hated cats, but allowed each of us to have a cat. Dad had a trained sheep collie, and we weren't allowed to play with him, but he made sure each of us had a mutt. I tried to catch owls and make pets of them, but they died."

"In the summertime we would get flat stones and use them for dishes. I remember catching a mouse in a trap and I put it on the plate, tail and all, and that was my meat." (Cecilia Murphy, Read, Ontario)

In Nova Scotia, Esther McDonell and her sisters and brother play-acted:

We played house all the time. We should have been a drama group because we were always someone else. I was Aunt Marj, and this one was Grandma, and the dolls would be cousins. I don't want to be Grandma any more, I want to be Aunt Marj.

The neighbour kids lived a mile away, so you played with family. We had weddings. One cousin and my brother were five or six years old. We put them in dresses, and they carried ferns. It gave us a chance to dress up, and we got the idea looking at pictures of weddings. They were about the only pictures around.

What her brother thought of it is not on record.
Some farm people claim they were never into mischief as

children because they worked too hard to have time for it, but the record suggests otherwise. Farm children had as many opportunities to get into trouble as their city counterparts, and they had a richer trove of raw materials to work with.

At Halloween we did things to annoy people. We'd take a big farm wagon and take it apart and heave it up on the barn roof. The farmer would have to get the neighbours to come and take it down. The less you made of it, the less harm was done.

We'd get in the pig pen and grab a young pig and throw it through a window, or shove a hen in a window. There was a lot of squawking and feathers flying. (Arnold Bent, Belleisle, Nova Scotia)

Clarence Read and his friends in Carvil, Ontario, also took advantage of Halloween, but the consequences one night were not quite what they expected.

We used to raise a row on Halloween pushing back-houses around. We pushed one over once and one of my friends wound up down there on his hands and knees in the hole, and had to go home and change. We didn't steal or break things. We worked harder at night than we did in the daytime, and then we had to go put it all back the next day. Everyone knew who it was.

I was in trouble most of the time. I had an old billy-goat, and he and I got into fights. I guess I smelled like a billy-goat. He could put you down in a hurry. Mother had a rockery in the lawn, in a circular drive. She looked out one day and the old billy-goat was just shaking the dirt off her prize maple. She took a rake and chased him and he went through the fence and turned and blahed at her, and she stopped.

"We played croquet and trained horse, played piano, played cards, and there was a lot of visiting." (Margaret Dixon, Parkman, Saskatchewan)

The organized games were at school, where there were enough kids, and they were the old games, games you could play whether there were only two of you, or a gang—hopscotch and jacks, marbles and anti-I-over. You needed two teams to play that, taking turns throwing a ball over the school roof and tagging opponents until one team had no players left. Baseball was a favourite, as improvised as hockey, with taped-up balls and home-made bats. You chose up sides, and usually the little kids played the outfield.

There were no highly organized leagues, but there was

Previous page: Children work quite hard on Halloween tipping over outhouses and putting heavy equipment in trees and on roofs, only to be called upon to straighten them up or take them down on November 1. CLARINGTON MUSEUMS/CLARKE MUSEUM AND ARCHIVES, KIRBY, ONTARIO/974.37.1D

Home-made wagons were constructed out of boxes and wheels from defunct vehicles. They worked fine.
ANNE STEWART, ALBERTA

Softball was the number one in summer, as was basketball. If the weather was bad, we played indoor games. The Wilkie Bowling Club gave me two sets of bowling pins for the students at Phippen. We padded the front of the room beneath the blackboards with heavy cardboard, chose up teams, and, using a softball for a bowling ball, we bowled all winter when the weather was unfit to go outside. (Madge Brathen, Saskatchewan)

interschool rivalry: "At our school every kid from grade one up played on the school baseball team, and you'd play other schools. Then six or eight schools had a sports day every year, competing. We'd practise exercise drills every day for two months, and we'd all dress the same and be judged on our drills, and it looked good."

Indoor games were checkers and crokinole, snakes and ladders and parcheesi, card games like snap, old maid, and fish. There was gossip—whispering a secret around a circle and giggling at the difference between what the first person said and the last one heard.

There were quiet times at home, when children made scrapbooks out of catalogues and magazines, with a paste made of flour and water and a pinch of salt. Magazines printed paper dolls and clothes to cut out. Some mothers kept a small cache of things like that against the days when the children were down with the measles or colds.

Quiet time for some families meant reading:

I joined the library in Cobourg. Dad always insisted on a half hour after we were through a meal, and I would read

my books. At bedtime I would take and put my apron around the stovepipe so the light wouldn't shine through downstairs. If I didn't, my mother would yell up, "Frances, put your book down." (Frances Davey, Cobourg, Ontario)

When you got a little older, you could look for amusement farther afield: "When I was about eleven, we'd hitchhike into Cloverdale, seven miles away, to see a movie. People didn't worry about kids." (John Rygh, Port Kells, British Columbia)

"In Carbon we saw Snow White. It was free, I think, in the Scout hall. I was about seven or eight, and thrilled to go. I can remember a neighbour would take a load in to see the parade in Calgary. We couldn't go; we didn't have any money." (Irma Lowry, Carbon, Alberta)

Movies had appeared in a puff of steam at about the turn of the century. Rhodes C.M. Grant, in *Horse and Buggy Days in Martintown, 1900–1940*, wrote:

It's hard now to imagine the effect on people to whom a magic lantern show had been a wonder. I saw my first

The cat looks surprisingly calm carried into a game by a mystery man in dark glasses. ANNE STEWART, ALBERTA movie when I was nine or ten, in the Wonder-land in Martintown, Quebec. A huge steam locomotive came rushing from the back of the screen straight at me. If my father hadn't grabbed my collar, I would have jumped up and run out.

Chances are that this child, off to a movie about 1916, saw D.W. Griffith's *Birth of a Nation.*

Movies were shown in Arcola, Saskatchewan, in an upstairs hall. I remember going with my friend Billie McGraw, who wore a peanut scoop, a cap with a small visor. There was one about a war. They made it more exciting by red colouring on the films when they showed cannon fire. Kids could go in for a nickel, a very small silver coin that it was very easy to lose between the cracks in the wooden sidewalk. (Queen Macdonald, Arcola, Saskatchewan)

If a boy has a bucket and there's lots of dirt, he can amuse himself for hours, like this young man in 1930s Quebec. MCCORD MUSEUM, NOTMAN ARCHIVES, MONTREAL/MP 10/92 (63)

We used to walk to Jacquet River, which was five or six miles away, just to go, maybe to skate, maybe, when we were older, to watch the boys play a hockey game. The first movies we saw were in the church hall, and they were silent. I remember when I was thirteen, in about 1938, my dad and my two brothers had been working, and they took me to town and bought me a new coat and a watch. We were so used to hand-me-downs, that was my first new coat. And we went to a movie, a talking movie, and I thought it was wonderful. (Florence Thompson, Black Point, New Brunswick)

Sandstorms, like this one in Saskatchewan, as well as hail, drought, and grasshoppers added to the economic depression of the 1930s, creating terrible hardship for farm families in large areas of the Prairie Provinces. ARCHIVES OF THE UNITED CHURCH OF CANADA, VICTORIA UNIVERSITY, TORONTO/92.195C

Hard Times and New Developments

FARM CHILDREN SHARED THE HARD TIMES OF the 1930s Depression. Shoes were expensive, so they went barefoot or wore ill-fitting rubber boots. They saved their best clothes, most of those cut down and made over, for school and church. They missed school sometimes because there was no money to pay taxes or teachers, even when the teachers worked for a pittance. Still, many of them say they didn't feel poor: "We weren't a poor family, though we'd be considered poor by today's standards." (Arnold Bent, Belleisle, Nova Scotia)

Most people claim the situation was eased by the fact that they shared the predicament with everyone they knew; as long as the basic necessities of life were met, they felt they were doing fine: "We were all in the same boat. We were never hungry; we were never cold." (Nazla Dane, Indian Head, Saskatchewan)

The inevitable sacrifices that had to be made were met, in general, with a certain stoicism, and there were always alternatives: "I never felt hard up. I only went to high school for three months. Dad couldn't afford it, so I took grade ten

Many people stayed on their farms during the 1930s, eking out a living and waiting for better times. ARCHIVES OF THE UNITED CHURCH OF CANADA, VICTORIA UNIVERSITY, TORONTO/92.195C

by correspondence." (Margaret Dixon, Parkman, Saskatchewan)

The self-sufficiency of the family farm allowed families to consider themselves well off:

We had about forty acres, and there were ten kids. Father fished for lobster in February and March. We raised all our own vegetables. We had two cows, a couple of calves, a pig, and about thirty hens. It fed the family during the 1930s. We were well off because we raised everything we needed. We had times when we didn't have a dollar, but we seemed to live all right. The main thing we had to buy was kerosene and molasses. The local store wouldn't give any credit. (Ben Goodwin, Cape Sable, Nova Scotia)

And a lack of money, and even hard feelings, rarely prevented anyone from lending a helping hand:

Nobody had any money, but it was a community. There was lots of squabbling, lots of politics; you could hate a neighbour's guts, but you'd go in and help. (John Rygh, Port Kells, British Columbia)

On the Prairies, the plague years that came with the economic woes of the Depression were a farmer's nightmare, and have become a symbol of the Depression across Canada. There were crop failures, grasshoppers, black windstorms that tore away the topsoil and left behind layers of choking dust; there were violent, frightening hailstorms that destroyed crops year after year, killing some small livestock outright and contributing, with the duststorms, to the slow starvation of others.

The family called this shot "after a hard winter," as animals and people hope the snow keeps melting in 1935 Alberta. ANNE STEWART, ALBERTA

During the Depression, many people who had cars or trucks couldn't afford to run them, and the horse kept at its work. ANNE STEWART, ALBERTA

A prairie woman remembers her mother standing at the end of the kitchen table watching her family eat, protesting that she wouldn't eat with them because she wasn't hungry.

Irma Lowry from Carbon, Alberta, says her family's crop was hailed out seven years in a row:

> My dad bought fifty-seven panes of glass one year. I remember the year I was ten. A storm hit at 6:00, and we ran for shelter in the far bedroom. Dad put tarpaper over the windows to protect them. Another year Mom was baking bread and she put the pan of dough under the bed so it wouldn't get glass in it.

Spectacular though the hailstorms could be, the dust-storms were far more common, and just as destructive in their own way:

> A duststorm would come just a rollin' up and as black as black, just like a black blizzard, and it would get into the doors and windows. You just stayed in the house until it was over. Sweep what you could, but then you'd have to scrub it all and wash everything. Ah—it did make a mess.
> (Inez Anderson, Gladys Ridge, Alberta)

But if the Prairies suffered most, the whole country was learning to make do in the 1930s. During those years, Cana-

> "After a hailstorm that had covered the ground, I took my sand pail and shovel and filled it with marble-sized hail."

dian farm income dropped to less than half of what it had been in 1928. In 1932, an average Ontario family farm netted $147.26, 70 percent of which was income in kind. People put the cars away and dusted off the buggies:

> Our mode of transportation was horse and wagon or horse and sled. My dad did have a car before the Depression, but when the Depression came, the car went into the garage and stayed there. But we were happy. (Maxine Keith, Rimbey, Alberta)

No one could afford new clothing, but the ingenuity of farm women kept their families adequately covered, if not perfectly presentable. Everyone remembers those handy flour sacks:

> My brother got some clothes from the family in England. Mother made us dresses out of flour bags. We wore those to school, then went home and put on rags. But we kids were happy, and we learned to do without. I'm that way now—why buy something if you don't need it? (Irma Lowry, Carbon, Alberta)

One-hundred-pound flour bags were used for many things—clothes, curtains, pillowcases, and tea towels; five made a sheet.

There was more bartering, and people turned a hand to whatever was available to help get along: "You took a pig to the store and came home with flour and tea. Dad cut firewood and pulp to sell. He fished in the spring and you salted herring for the winter, and you salted pork for the summer." (Florence Thompson, Black Point, New Brunswick)

Hitching a ride in time-honoured fashion in 1930s Alberta. ANNE STEWART, ALBERTA

In the West, some families who lived outside the dustbowl area managed to maintain their livestock and were lucky enough to find markets for their goods: "Sheep saw our family through the 1930s. Wool prices were good, and Dad always said that's what saw them through. (Maxine Keith, Rimbey, Alberta)

Though times were tough, many people have fond memories of special occasions:

They did buy me a bicycle, and my grandpa had an old car with a rumble seat, and we loved to ride in that. We had an uncle who came from the States, and he used to take us around to the other side of the island to Clark's Harbor and buy us ice cream. (Ben Goodwin, Cape Sable, Nova Scotia)

The Depression slowed and even set back development. Those who had phones and electricity tried to keep them, though not everyone could. A United Church survey recorded 1,990 telephones in Manitoba in 1924. By 1931 the **number had** dropped to 1,613, and by 1932, to 1,490. Ingenious **farmers** found a way to attach telephone lines to wire fences so they could at least reach a neighbour. The improvisation was good for about a mile.

We had an extension phone because Mother was not well. My uncle had a phone because he was a retail farmer for milk—he took it to the station. My brother hooked up a line across the fields, so when they turned it on, it would give us the phone across the field. (Esther McDonell, Enfield County, Nova Scotia)

Ontario Hydro promoted electric power about 1912 with the Adam Beck Circus, which travelled the province showing people appliances like separators and washing-machines that could be run by electricity to cut down the work for everyone. CORPORATE ARCHIVES, ONTARIO HYDRO/HP670

This photo of a 1927 farm kitchen was part of the promotion for electric power, showing lighting, a toaster, iron, and hotplate. No refrigerator or stove is in evidence, though. CITY OF VAUGHAN ARCHIVES/M993.20.107

In 1931, about 17 percent of farms had electricity or gas, and it was pretty exciting when it was first installed. "Not until after our daughter was born in 1930 did we have the electric. She was old enough to run around and put the lights on." (Grace Arthur, Alnwick Township, Ontario) The lights might mean only one in the barn, one in the kitchen, and one in the upstairs hall, but having electricity meant wonderful labour-saving possibilities for the future—power to run a saw, a milking machine, a separator, and eventually a washing-machine.

Electricity had begun to inch along rural roads in the 1920s; the Depression slowed its spread until into the 1950s, though it was just too useful to stop altogether. In the early days, some potential customers were suspicious: "My folks got hydro around 1928. You had to have three subscribers to the mile, and Dad and another neighbour paid a third neighbour's fee to get it. She was kind of an old biddy." (Frances Davey, Cobourg, Ontario)

Radio had also sparked into life in the 1920s, when household sets operated on batteries. As in any era, it was often the children who grasped the new toy with the most enthusiasm.

I built myself a short-wave radio. It had two tubes and

batteries, and had a four-foot aerial of thick copper wire. I had a how-to magazine, and bought the parts mail order from Toronto—two knobs, batteries, wood. The whole thing cost about $5.00. I got Radio Station DJB in Berlin when the Olympics were on in 1938. I could get London and Australia. People talked about the places they reached. You could send a postcard to a distant radio station and ask for a confirmation of what you had listened to.

Eventually the family had a Westinghouse radio with three batteries and two tubes. We cut down a tree and put it up in the backyard so we could string an aerial, and we listened with earphones. In the 1930s you could get stories and operas. (Tim Dickson, St. Joseph Island, Ontario)

You could also get farm broadcasts and weather reports, and there was *The Happy Gang,* Canadian writer and broadcaster Kate Aitken, Canadian country star Don Messer and his Islanders, not to mention Jack Benny, *Fibber McGee and Molly*, and *The Lone Ranger*. If you didn't have a radio of your own, you went somewhere else to listen. Smart salesmen left

When Foster Hewitt was first the voice of "Hockey Night in Canada," radios had earphones. If you put the earphones in a metal washtub, his voice was amplified and the whole family could sit around and listen. COLLECTION OF MIKE SABIDASH

radios in barber-shops and general stores. *Hockey Night in Canada* began in 1927, giving Canadian kids a new set of heroes and ambitions. If you put the radio earphones in a galvanized tub, everyone in the family could hear the game.

We listened to Foster Hewitt broadcasting the hockey games on Saturday night, and it really was a hot-stove league. We'd all go sit around the old box stove in the general store at Carlisle. (Gordon Bennett, Carlisle, Ontario)

The United Church survey, commenting on the social value of radio, noted sadly that the number of radios in use also dropped during the Depression.

It must be remembered, however, that in the rural areas the possession of a radio does not necessarily imply its use. Being dependent on batteries for use,

there is no doubt that hard times have made it necessary for many people to economize and so discontinue the use of this gift of modern science which has done so much to banish the sense of isolation and winter tediousness from farm life.

We had a big power-pack radio. We didn't listen to it often, and when the battery died, we couldn't afford to replace it. (Maxine Keith, Rimbey, Alberta)

Mary Grannon was Just Mary, originator and voice of a popular CBC radio program that went on to be a success on early television. CBC ARCHIVES/61-417-24

In the meantime, broadcasting expanded and technology improved. The CBC increased and improved its programming for children and extended it into the schools, taking rich new resources in entertainment and connections with the outside world into homes and schools that could hear it. In 1939, the CBC announced it would run a children's serial called *The Magical Voyage*, conceived "with the objective of getting away from the blood and thunder type of broadcast which has proved so objectionable to many parents and adult education groups." That same year, *Just Mary* began broadcasting for the very young. She would make the transition to television in the 1950s. The French network had *Etait un Fois*, fairy tales and folklore—*La Marmaille, Yvan l'Intrépide*.

National school broadcasts began in Nova Scotia and British Columbia in 1941, and in co-operation with the provincial Departments of Education, spread quickly to other provinces. Wide-ranging programs included *My Canada, The Way of Free Men*, a weekly news review, and *Shakespeare Highlights*. They had a greeting, sung to the tune of "At Boules Ball," a French-Canadian folksong.

> Attention everyone,
> Our broadcast has begun.
> To brighten work today
> We use the radio way.
>
> Welcome listeners, welcome to our radio class

> Today, today,
> We use the radio way
> To brighten work today
> In music, word and play.

The approach of World War II, ending the Depression, brought its own shortages, some of them tragic, as it took young men and women off the farm and out of rural schools, into war work in the cities, and into the armed forces. Back home, the younger ones worked a little harder on the farm.

During World War II, Canadians had ration books with stamps in them that had to be used to buy items like butter and meat, which were in short supply.

By 1939, a slick Hydro Travel Shop was on the road in rural Ontario to show farm families what electricity could do. In many parts of rural Canada, though, electric power wouldn't be available until after World War II ended in 1945. CORPORATE ARCHIVES, ONTARIO HYDRO/HP951

"When the boys were called to the services, off they went. One brother, my sister, and myself were left to help my parents."

Government projects helped equip farmers, who were urged to produce more and to put more acreage into crops. A limited number of small tractors were made available, for example, and late in the war, combines were built for a Harvest Brigade that started in Texas and cut a swath northward into the Prairies to harvest a bumper wheat crop. But for the most part, farmers, like everyone else, did what they could with rationed supplies.

Children's work was encouraged and its value recognized. Ontario, for example, had a Farm Service Force with a Children's Brigade to recruit young people to work on farms, especially at harvest time, and took them out of school to do it. "They had a little project when George Drew was premier. You could be excused from school to help the farmers. I went and picked berries for a week and got a certificate." (Margaret Crawford, Erieau, Ontario)

Children in both town and country schools were mobilized to do their share of war work, raising money to buy war stamps and bonds, collecting salvage to be recycled into war materials, knitting, sewing, making splints and bandages.

We had whist drives and crokinole drives held at the school for the war effort. We had such good times getting together like that. On Friday afternoons we knit for the Red Cross in school, made socks for the soldiers, with supervision from the teacher. We knitted khaki and big blue scarves, and I swear no one ever wore them, the knitting was terrible. (Margaret Dixon, Parkman, Saskatchewan)

There was concern about school standards as teachers left their classrooms for the armed forces and for better paid war work. A Newfoundland Department of Education report stated the case, though there was little that could be done about it.

Conditions arising from the war have greatly increased the difficulties under which our educational service is operating. Many of our competent teachers have temporarily withdrawn from the profession. The number of ungraded teachers employed this year is much greater than at any other time in our history, and these conditions will probably continue for the duration of the war. While our ungraded and inexperienced teachers will discharge their duties conscientiously, they cannot be expected to give a service equal to that rendered by the experienced group.

Radios opened windows on a wider world for farm families, including children, as special programs were produced for them. ARCHIVES OF THE UNITED CHURCH OF CANADA, VICTORIA UNIVERSITY, TORONTO/92.195C

Radio truly came into its own during World War II, bringing the war closer to rural people who, until then, had had little access to news beyond their own horizons. "We started to listen to Gabriel Heater, the American newscaster. We had

not been much aware of the rest of the country, few of us had newspapers regularly. We didn't get news from British Columbia or the States. For instance, there were Japanese working on farms near Windsor, Ontario, during the war, and we kids had no idea why they were there." (Margaret Crawford, Erieau, Ontario) They were, of course, some of the people who had been uprooted from their homes near the British Columbia coast.

The CBC did broadcasts from England, carrying greetings from young Canadian servicemen stationed there. A Canadian wartime serial called *L for Lanky* dramatized the adventures of a fictional crew of an RCAF Lancaster bomber, and was eagerly listened to by kids.

Real airplanes, from training bases, were appearing in home skies, causing great excitement. "I remember phoning the neighbours the first time a plane went over. There were about eight kids in our school, near Camp Shiloh. Every time we heard a plane, we'd run out the door, and the teacher would come with us. The pilots would dip their wings." Even in remote areas, children practised air-raid drills and studied silhouettes so they could identify enemy aircraft. (Margaret Dixon, Parkman, Saskatchewan)

When it was over there was a burst of joy across the country, and some wonder. "In Summerside, on V-E Day, there was a great parade, and I remember thinking, what do they mean by peace? What would that be like?" (Dorothy Johnson, Eldon, Prince Edward Island)

Facing page: Ponies were more sure-footed transportation than bikes on bumpy rural roads like Rhubarb Lane, which led to the Red River in Manitoba. PROVINCIAL ARCHIVES OF MANITOBA, MARTHA KNAPP COLLECTION 77/N17404

End of an Era

*T*HE WAR HAD BROUGHT PROSPERITY TO FARMERS, as to many other Canadians, and its aftermath would bring great change. For a time, there was a feeling of affluence and progress, as the combination of available money and new technology made itself felt. For farmers, it was a whole new world.

The life of farm communities began to change. Telephones had brought them closer for a while; then other elements broke them apart. Once bastions of self-sufficiency, farms gradually produced less food just for the family and fewer household and personal items, as it became easier and cheaper to go to town to buy bread and sweaters. "We were about a mile from the local store, and suddenly, when you have a car, you go to town instead, which was seventeen miles away." (Florence Thompson, Black Point, New Brunswick) The consumer gap between town and country began to close.

We finally got a big deForest radio; one of my brothers

The horses were Frank and Kate, and in 1939 they were on the verge of being replaced by tractors. RUTH LAWLEY, NORTH SYDNEY, NOVA SCOTIA

Once cars and trucks were available, thousands of horses disappeared almost overnight from Canadian farms. RUTH LAWLEY, NORTH SYDNEY, NOVA SCOTIA

bought it, and we'd have good music on at night. Another brother lived in town. He would buy a box of cornflakes, and we all used to go to his place to have a feed of cornflakes, and that was so good. When we got bought bread, that was really something. (Frances Raityn, Beausejour, Manitoba)

The old conditions began to take on an aura of nostalgia for people no longer putting up with them. "We got electricity after the war; until then we had a battery radio and oil lamps. When I was first working in Bathurst, my friends wanted to come up and visit the farm, because it was roughing it." (Florence Thompson, Black Point, New Brunswick)

Increasing mechanization brought enormous changes both economic and social to the family farm. It affected the size of farms and the population who worked them, as more acreage could be handled with fewer people; it changed the nature of farm work, how quickly it could be done, and altered family dynamics in the once-fixed division of labour; and it meant, sadly to many, the virtual disappearance of the horse—possibly the most enduring symbol of the early family farm—from the rural landscape.

Farmers had started to mechanize through the 1930s, but

it was slowed by the Depression and during the war, when you couldn't get gas. Then in '45, when you could get fuel, people started to cut down the number of horses they kept. On grain farms, as long as they cut grain with a binder the horses were useful, but the thresher and binder were superseded by combines after the war, that did everything in one operation. (Gordon Bennett, Carlisle, Ontario)

> "We had a phone, but didn't get electricity until the 1950s. After the war there were more tractors, and you could get a lot more done." (Maxine Keith, Rimbey, Alberta)

Although the advent of machinery offered speed and labour-saving opportunities in many areas of farm life, there were still some chores best done the old way: "By the 1940s, everything was mechanized. We still used a team to spray the fruit trees, because they could get closer, but there were fewer animals to feed, and Dad wouldn't allow kids near the machinery." (Margaret Crawford, Erieau, Ontario)

Some dads did; they needed the help.

For farm children the main difference in work at home was how things were done; the chores were still there: "In some ways the smaller tractors lengthened the time a child would work. A ten-, eleven-, twelve-year old could operate a tractor, all you had to do was push buttons. Women could operate them, too, where they did not usually drive the horses to plough." (Gordon Bennett, Carlisle, Ontario)

Ruth Lawley, in Cape Breton, Nova Scotia, notes:

By the time the war was over, we didn't have horses any more. We probably did three to five acres of carrots and ten of potatoes. Dad shipped a lot of it to Newfoundland by boat. We also had a milk delivery route, and I was driving the truck by the time I was thirteen. The local chief of police knew me, but he just looked the other way.

> "People would be shocked to realize that twelve-year-old boys were driving three-ton trucks and combines." (Frances Raityn, Beausejour, Manitoba)

From the earliest days of mechanization, most farm children simply grew up with the machinery, and it was taken for granted that they'd drive it as soon as their feet could reach the pedals. Tracy Jennings, growing up near Blenheim, Ontario, after the war, said,

From the time I was about five, I would sit on Dad's lap in the tractor, and from about age nine, I could drive it,

Facing page: Children helping with a harvest during World War I.
PROVINCIAL ARCHIVES OF MANITOBA, MARTHA KNAPP COLLECTION 38/N17379

though he'd be in the same field and watch you. He'd do the ploughing, and I'd come along and cultivate it. When Dad was picking corn, he'd keep us away from that machine, because it was dangerous—a neighbour had lost an arm.

Despite the machines, however, farm chores still required plenty of manual labour. Tracy Jennings continues:

As soon as we got home from school we had to get the work clothes on. We were farming a hundred acres, oats, corn, and soya beans. I'd go down to a neighbour's field and pick tomatoes, go pick strawberries on an aunt and uncle's farm, and then come home and hoe down the garden.

You had to work right beside the men. You'd lift up the bales of hay and put them on the wagon, and unload them up in the mow. When a bale got up into the mow, you had to walk it to the end, and it was hot up there, and dusty.

Just as they drove horses, farm children, even the very young, learned to drive trucks and tractors like this 1940 model Ford Ferguson. RUTH LAWLEY, NORTH SYDNEY, NOVA SCOTIA

"But," she added, "my folks worked a lot harder than my sister and me, because they had to do the thrashing and put up the stooks."

By 1941, about 65 percent of Ontario farms still had horses, but most also had a tractor and a truck.

We had horses in Alberta pretty well up into the '40s. The first tractor was a big deal, a little Case tractor. I'd run the tractor when I was about twelve, and Dad would do the bundle, because I couldn't reach down far enough.

Things became more modern. Recreation was the same, people still got together to make their fun, but we had horses, and suddenly they were gone. We had Jeeps after the war. It was so odd not to have your horses to work with and ride. (Maxine Keith, Rimbey, Alberta)

There were factories set up to process horse meat for export, but on some farms the horses were allowed to live out their lives like old friends, doing an occasional job, said Pearl Bennett of Carlisle,

In postwar British Columbia, egg collection changed from the hunt underneath the barn. NATIONAL ARCHIVES OF CANADA/PA 159658

Ontario, "because farmers appreciated their horses; they didn't send them to the glue factory until they had to. They were part of the family." There were farmers who kept a team long after they had mechanized, simply because they enjoyed having them.

> You needed a chore team in Alberta for the winter, but gradually, even there, you used a tractor to pull a stone-boat. We were still riding horseback, and we kept the horses and pastured them out until they died of old age. (Maxine Keith, Rimbey, Alberta)

Still, the work moved much faster when machinery was used. Gordon Bennett observed:

> The average family farm was about one hundred to two hundred acres then, and they didn't get any bigger for a while. Small tractors were marketed; there was a Ferguson system. You could attach implements to them, and they were plenty for a one- or two-man farm. With a team of horses and a walking plough you'd get one or two acres done in a day; with a tractor you'd skim through it, depending on how many furrow ploughs you used. At that time, two or three was normal.

Mechanization did more than change and speed up chores, however: "Gradually, as people got mechanized, they had to worry about cash flow. You couldn't afford to work at your neighbour's grain while yours was waiting. If you have your own machinery, you don't have to wait, and you start to become a larger unit. The inter-dependence began to go."

So did the sons and daughters: "As they grew up they weren't needed, because you could handle the farm without as many people. Once a farm could support two or three families, but not any more, so the kids had to leave." (Margaret Dixon, Parkman, Saskatchewan)

Canadian Federation of Agriculture statistics show an enormous drop in farm population over the fifty-year period from the 1930s, when the decrease started, through the 1950s, when it began to accelerate, and into the 1980s. In 1931, about 32 percent of Canadians were still farming, but by 1986 the number had plummeted to 4 percent, in a country that had once been overwhelmingly agricultural. At the same time, the size of the average farm had grown from 200 to 575 acres, and a quarter of it was rented.

Margaret Dixon said her area in Saskatchewan "is still farmland, but there is much more broken and cropped, much bigger farms and bigger machinery. It's just a vicious circle. You need more land to pay for the machinery, and bigger machinery to work the land; it's a real circle."

Facing page: In 1947, children at the Pemberton School in British Columbia appear to be eating ice-cream from a store, unthinkable a few years earlier. BRITISH COLUMBIA ARCHIVES AND RECORDS SERVICE/46531

The rural school was both a symbol and a cause of change. Its days were numbered after the war. A move to consolidation had begun as far back as the 1920s, but had met with stiff resistance. The early consolidations only brought together two or three school districts or sections to form three- and four-room schools. The atmosphere was not much different, nor did the children have vast distances to travel to them. To encourage the idea, the Macdonald Consolidated School Project underwrote the costs of schools in Middleton, Nova Scotia, Kingston, New Brunswick, Guelph, Ontario, and Hillsboro, Prince Edward Island, but they all died on the vine. People blamed it on costs, on distances, and the uncertainty of travel, but in fact, they failed because the farm communities didn't want to relinquish control.

Officials in every province promoted consolidation, pointing out the advantages in economy and in the improvement in quality of education in schools where children could be grouped by age and given more individual attention. The arguments cut no ice. And then, like other development, consolidation was stalled by depression and war, and opponents got a reprieve.

After the war, education departments sold the idea to the

The spotted pig is clearly contemplating the rattling, back-firing symbol of the beginning of the end of an old way of life. MADGE BRATHEN, SASKATCHEWAN

children, taking them into town schools where there were gyms and auditoriums, labs and cafeterias, home ec kitchens and manual training rooms, and indoor washrooms. In one area, they eased the process by giving the rural children their year-end exams early, then getting them to help move supplies and equipment from their local schools to the new building in the nearby town, ready for the fall term. They adopted a one road, one bus policy, so that public school, Roman Catholic, and high school kids from the same neighbourhood came in together. But even so, the change took some doing. The last one-room schools didn't close until the 1960s, and by then, efficient roads and buses had made it inevitable.

The departure by bus every day to a separate life was a much different experience than hiking off down the back road to attend school with only your siblings and neighbours. However, the children quickly made friends in the town-based clubs and sports leagues they belonged to, and it wasn't long before it was taken for granted that farm kids would go on to high school just as their town friends did. "We had five sons, and they had a chance to go to school and get out." (Mary Burton, Vellore, Ontario)

Previous page: The outdoor bread oven has almost become the symbol of rural Quebec before the days of electricity. MCCORD MUSEUM, NOTMAN ARCHIVES, MONTREAL/MP 010/92(10)

Although the educational opportunities for farm kids were long overdue, the closure of the small rural schools had a devastating effect on the surrounding communities. Said Margaret Dixon, in Saskatchewan:

It made a profound difference, to the children, their families, and the community. We lost our little communities when the schools consolidated. When they closed, it put an end to neighbouring. It was at the country school that you'd have your dances, crokinole drives, Christmas concerts. Everything happened at the schools. Then when consolidation came, some were bused twenty miles, some went in another direction, they got involved in clubs in the towns, and it split up our communities.

She and others say the closeness is what they miss most about the farm life of their childhoods.

It was quite different. The roads weren't there, the money wasn't there. People didn't travel great distances.

There was time to do things, to enjoy things, and we did them together as a family. I was a bird-watcher, and there was time for my mother or my dad to come out to the bush and identify birds for me.

At night Mom or Dad would read poetry aloud, or Dad would turn off all the lights and we'd listen to a spooky radio program, and we did it together. We'd have weiner roasts and the whole neighbourhood would come.

There was a respect for nature, and we didn't break things, didn't destroy the land. There was so much beauty around. We children had our chores, but we took pride in that, in the fact that we were an important part of the unit.

For many children of the farm, the world of childhood has disappeared altogether, buried under concrete and suburban housing. Margaret Dixon sums it up for all of them: "The homes and the barns are gone, and city buses come right up to where I grew up with oil lamps and well water. I can hardly realize it's happened."

References

Akenson, Donald, ed. *Canadian Papers in Rural History*. Vols. 2, 5, 6. (Kinnear, Mary. *Do You Want Your Daughter to Marry a Farmer? Women's Work on the Farm, 1922, United Farm Women of Manitoba Survey*) Gananoque: Langdale Press, 1986.

Anderson, Allan. *Remembering the Farm*. Toronto: Macmillan of Canada, 1977.

Arthur, Peter. *Around Home*. Toronto: Musson Book Co. Ltd., 1925.

Bagnell, Kenneth. *The Little Immigrants*. Toronto: MacMillan of Canada, 1980.

Baird, LtCol. William T. *Seventy Years of New Brunswick Life*. 1890. Reprint Saint John, N.B.: St. Anne's Point Press, 1979.

Blandford, Percy W. *Old Farm Tools and Machinery*. Fort Lauderdale: Gale Research Co., 1976.

Bouchard, George. *Silhouettes of the Past in French Canada*. Trans. *Vieilles Choses Vieilles Gens*. Montreal and New York: Louis Carrier and Co. at the Mercury, 1928.

Bragg, Betty. "Among the Settlers on the Prairies." *Social Welfare,* June 1981.

Britnell, George, and Vernon Fowke. *Canadian Agriculture in War and Peace, 1935–45*. Stanford: Stanford University Press, 1962.

Brow, Prof. William. *The Farm Treasury, or The Science and Practice of Farming with Special Reference to Canada*. Canadian Home Series of Useful Books No. 2. Toronto, London, Brockville, and Saint John: J.S. Robertson and Bros., 1883.

Canadian 4-H Council. *Learn to Do by Doing: A History of the 4-H in Canada*. Ottawa, 1982.

Czumer, W.A. *Recollections about the Life of the First Ukrainian Settlers in Canada*. Edmonton: Canadian Institute of Ukrainian Studies, 1981.

Dickinson, Dr. George A. *The Country Boy*. Toronto: William Briggs, 1907.

Drummond, Ian M. *Progress Without Planning: The Economic History of Ontario from Confederation to the Second World War*. Ontario Historical Studies Series for the Government of Ontario. Toronto: University of Toronto Press, 1987.

Family in the Evolution of Agriculture, The. Ottawa: The Vanier Institute of the Family, 1968.

Ferguson, Carol, and Margaret Fraser. *A Century of Canadian Home Cooking*. Scarborough: Prentice Hall Canada, 1992.

Fowke, Vernon. *Canadian Agricultural Policy*. Toronto: University of Toronto Press, 1940.

Ganzevoort, Herman. *A Bittersweet Land*. Toronto: McClelland & Stewart, in association with the Secretary of State and the Canadian Government Publishing Centre, Supply and Services Canada, c. 1988.

Gill, E.A.W. *A Manitoba Chore Boy: The Experiences of a Young Emigrant Told from His Letters*. London: The Religious Tract Society, 1912.

Glazebrook, G.P. deT. *Life in Ontario: A Social History*. Toronto: University of Toronto Press, 1981.

Graham, W.H. *Greenbank: Country Matters in Nineteenth Century Ontario*. Peterborough: Broadview Press, 1988.

Grant, Rhodes C.M. *Horse and Buggy Days in Martintown, 1900–1940*. N.p., 1976.

Gray, James H. *Men Against the Desert*. Saskatoon: Western Producer Prairie Books, 1967.

Green, Gavin Hamilton. *The Old Log School and Huron Old Boys in Pioneer Days*. Goderich: Signal-Star Press, 1939.

Grier, Nina. "Letter to her father, Fort Macleod, Alberta, c. 1940." Glenbow Archives/M4 56.

Handbook for Girl Guides, or How Girls Can Help Build the Empire. London: Thomas Nelson and Sons, 1912.

Hilts, Rev. Joseph H. *Experiences of a Backwoods Preacher.* Toronto: William Briggs, 1887.

"In an Alien Community: The Experience of a Teacher in a Western Settlement." *Maclean's,* May 1, 1920.

Jenkins, Phil, and Ken Ginn. *Fields of Vision: A Journey to Canada's Family Farms.* Toronto: McClelland & Stewart, 1991.

Jones, David C. *Empire of Dust.* Edmonton: University of Alberta Press, 1987.

Kelso, J.J. "Children, Their Care, Training and Happiness as Future Citizens." Toronto: L.K. Cameron, 1910.

MacDermot, H.E., MD. *One Hundred Years of Medicine in Canada, 1867–1967.* Toronto: McClelland & Stewart, 1967.

MacEwan, Grant. *Between the Red and the Rockies.* Toronto: University of Toronto Press, 1952.

——. *Power for Prairie Plows.* Saskatoon: Western Producer Prairie Books, 1971.

McClung, Nellie. *Clearing in the West: An Autobiography.* Toronto: Thomas Allen and Son Ltd., 1976.

Parr, Joy. *Labouring Children: British Immigrant Apprentices to Canada, 1869–1924.* Montreal: McGill-Queen's University Press, 1980.

Popp, Mary. "Memoirs, 1897–1915." PAC MG31 H17.

Radcliffe, Stephen. "Memoirs of Stephen Radcliffe." PAC MG2 GA52.

Rasporich, Anthony W. *For a Better Life: A History of the Croatians in Canada.* Toronto: McClelland & Stewart, in co-operation with the Multiculturalism Directorate, Department of the Secretary of State, 1982.

Reamon, G. Elmore. *A History of Agriculture in Ontario.* Vol. II. Toronto: Ontario Ministry of Agriculture, 1970.

Royal Commission on Farm Machinery. *Technological Changes in Farm Machinery and Canadian Agriculture.* Canadian Agricultural Congress. Ottawa, 1969.

Sharpe, Errol. *A People's History of P.E.I.* Toronto: Steel Rail Publishing, 1976.

Shortt, S.E.D., ed. *Medicine in Canadian Society: Historical Perspectives.* (Sutherland, Neil. *To Create a Strong and Healthy Race: School Children in the Public Health Movement, 1880–1914*) Montreal: McGill-Queen's University Press, 1981.

Social Service Council of Canada, The. *Annual Report of the Committee on Immigration and Colonization.* "Canada's Child Immigrants." January 1925.

Sparling, Mary. *A Guide to Some Domestic Pioneer Skills.* Halifax: Nova Scotia Museum, 1972.

Statistics Canada. *The Farm Household.* Monographs, 1901, 1911, 1931, Census of Canada.

Stocki, Alexander. "Polish Pioneers of Good Faith and Bravery." PAC MG30 C124.

Stratton, Ira. "Now They Talk Canadian." *Maclean's,* September 1, 1920.

Watts, Prof. J.R. *Fifty Years of Rural Canada; Summary of Surveys.* Kingston: Queen's Theological College, 1933.

Wood, A.C. *Old Days on the Farm.* Toronto: McClelland & Stewart, 1918.

About the Author

*J*EAN COCHRANE was born in Chatham, Ontario, but grew up in New York State. She has lived in Toronto since 1953. Jean earned an honours B.A. in English from Mount Allison University, and went on to become the first women's editor at Canadian Press. At the Federation of Women Teachers' Associations of Ontario she wrote and helped produce a documentary film on the history of women's rights in Canada. As a result of that, she was asked to be general editor of a book series entitled Women in Canadian Life, and was also co-author of two acclaimed books in the series. She is the author of several books, including *The One-Room School in Canada,* and has published in numerous magazines and newspapers, including *Canadian Living, The Beaver, Discovery,* and others. Jean currently works in the Communications and Marketing Branch of the Ontario Ministry of Education and Training.

Library of Congress Cataloging-in-Publication Data is available.
A CIP catalogue record for this book is available from The British Library.
ISBN 0-7358-1849-5 (trade edition) 10 9 8 7 6 5 4 3 2 1
ISBN 0-7358-1850-9 (library edition) 10 9 8 7 6 5 4 3 2 1
Printed in Italy

For more information about our books, and the authors and artists
who create them, visit our web site: www.northsouth.com

Christophe Loupy

Don't Worry, Wags

Eve Tharlet

Translated by J. Alison James

A MICHAEL NEUGEBAUER BOOK
NORTH-SOUTH BOOKS / NEW YORK / LONDON

Wags was a worrier. When her brother and sisters played hide-and-seek, burrowing in the haystack, Wags hovered outside, worried that she'd be trapped beneath all that hay. When the other puppies scampered boldly into the farmyard each morning, Wags crept cautiously after them, worried about unexpected dangers that might have appeared there overnight. When the other puppies splashed happily in a big puddle, Wags circled it gingerly, worried that she might fall in and drown. Yes, Wags was a worrier.

One morning Mother called to her puppies, "Come on, hop up! We're going to the farmers' market!"
Wags watched her brother and sisters bound into the truck.
"Are you sure it's safe up there?" she asked.
"It's perfectly safe," said Mother. "Don't worry, Wags!"

The engine rumbled and coughed, and the truck bounced along. Wags shivered with fear. Would they all be bounced out onto the road? "How far is it?" she asked nervously. "What is a farmers' market? Is it dangerous?" Mother laughed. "Don't worry, Wags," she said. "The market is fun. And it's not dangerous if you stay right with me."

The market was incredible—so big
and bright and busy. Wags followed
along behind her family.

Suddenly Wags stopped. She stuck her nose in the air.
Ooh! Aah! The smells! Wags looked around and saw
a mountain of sausages. She saw a giant ham.
Everything smelled delicious.
Then she saw the butcher with his knife.
She hurried to catch up to her family.

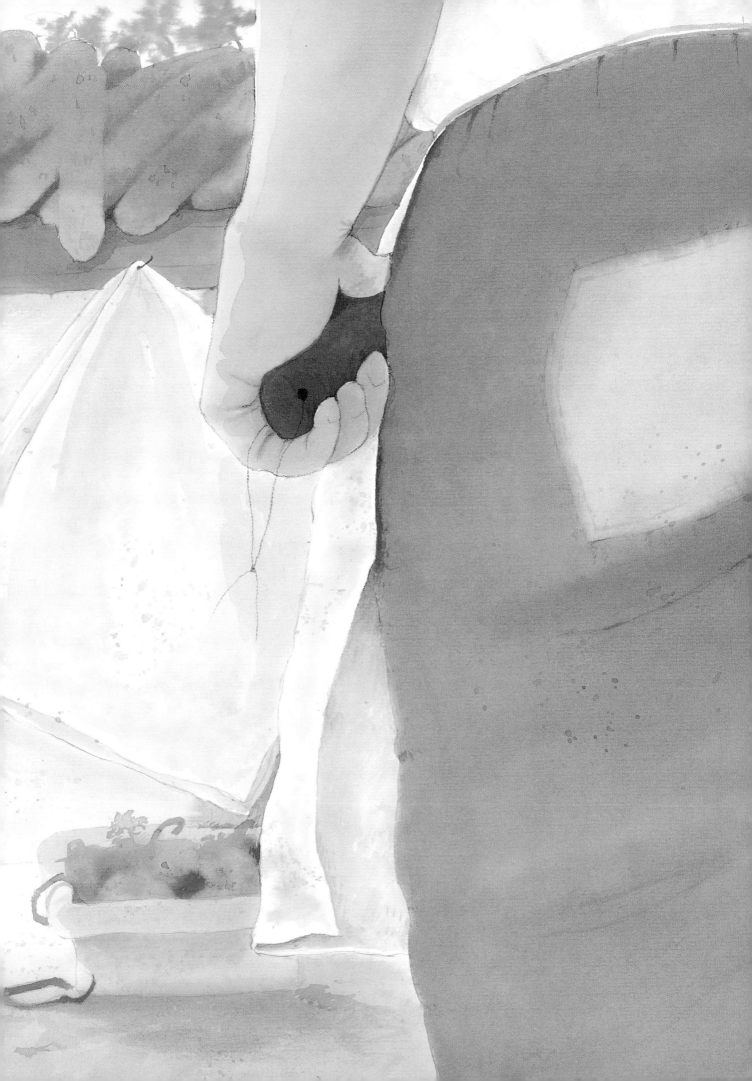

But where *were* they? Wags
looked left and right. All she
could see were legs—hundreds
of legs walking this way and that.
Dangerous legs that could
step on a little puppy.

Wags cried out, "Mother, Father,
where are you? *Arf! Arf! Arooouuu!*"
But nobody answered.

All alone, Wags wandered around looking for her family. She saw a nanny goat with her baby kid. Wags wanted to be with *her* mother. She started to cry.

"Who are you and why are you crying?" asked the nanny goat.

"I'm Wags and I lost my mother," said Wags sniffling.

"Don't worry, Wags. She can't be far," said the goat. "And she is surely looking for you. Why don't you climb up on something tall so you can get a better view?"

Wags saw a big stone fountain. It was tall. She scrambled and kicked with all four legs and pulled herself up over the edge. *SPLASH!* Wags landed headfirst in the water. She sputtered and climbed out, shaking herself dry. What a dangerous fountain, she thought.

Meow! Meow! A scruffy cat jumped gracefully onto the edge of the fountain. "Who are you? Are you looking for fish?" he asked. "I'm Wags and I'm looking for my family," Wags whimpered.

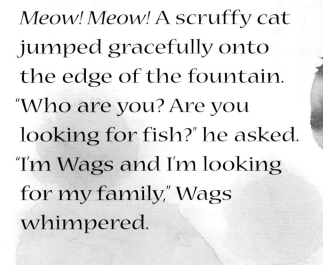

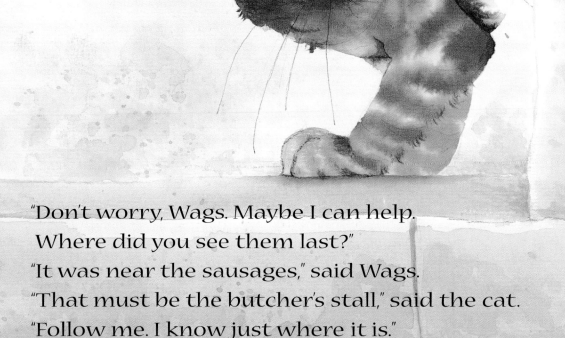

"Don't worry, Wags. Maybe I can help. Where did you see them last?" "It was near the sausages," said Wags. "That must be the butcher's stall," said the cat. "Follow me. I know just where it is."

The sausages were there. The ham was there. The butcher was there. But Wags's family was not there. Wags trembled forlornly. "What will I do if I never find them?"

"Now, now. Don't worry, Wags," said the cat. "Wait here while I look for a policeman to help."

Wags sighed and sat down to wait.

A string of sausages dangled over her head. The smell teased her nose and made her tummy growl with hunger. Cautiously, Wags licked one. It was oh, so delicious! She took just a nibble. Mmmm. She took a bite. Before she knew it, the string of sausages slipped off the table. That caught the butcher's eye and he began to shout.
Terrified, Wags ran for her life.

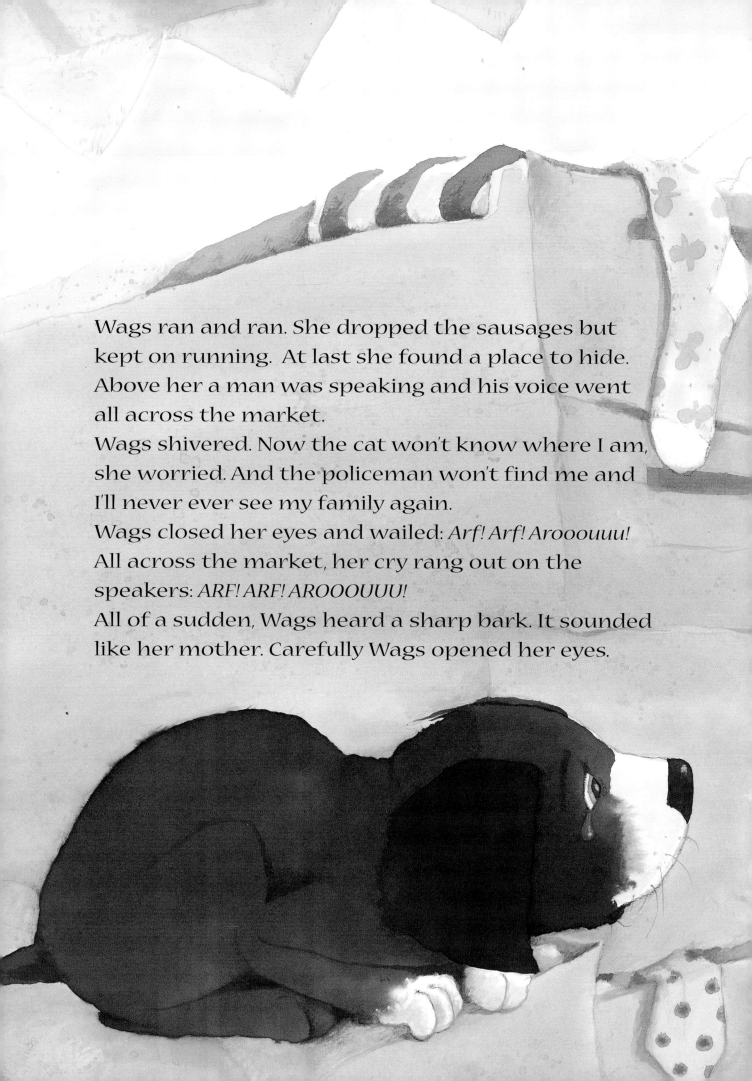

Wags ran and ran. She dropped the sausages but kept on running. At last she found a place to hide. Above her a man was speaking and his voice went all across the market.

Wags shivered. Now the cat won't know where I am, she worried. And the policeman won't find me and I'll never ever see my family again.

Wags closed her eyes and wailed: *Arf! Arf! Arooouuu!*

All across the market, her cry rang out on the speakers: *ARF! ARF! AROOOUUU!*

All of a sudden, Wags heard a sharp bark. It sounded like her mother. Carefully Wags opened her eyes.

It *was* her mother—and her father and brother and sisters, too!

"Don't worry, Wags," said Mother, kissing her softly on the head. "We're here now."

"We looked everywhere for you," said Father. "And then we heard you calling."

Wags stayed right between her parents for the rest of the day. The market was fun and not at all dangerous. They found the cat and thanked him, and later they found a long string of sausages that had been thrown away behind the butcher's stall. What a delicious snack!

When it was time to go home, Wags was the first one on the truck. "Can I go again next time?" she asked. "Don't worry, Wags," said Mother. "We'll never go anywhere without you!"